What Makes Heirloom Plants So Great?

NUMBER FORTY-ONE

W. L. Moody Jr. Natural History Series

Victor Z. Martin
2003

What Makes Heirloom Plants So Great?

Old-fashioned Treasures to Grow, Eat & Admire

JUDY BARRETT

Art by Victor Z. Martin

TEXAS A&M UNIVERSITY PRESS   COLLEGE STATION

Library of Congress Cataloging-in-Publication Data

Barrett, Judy, 1945–
  What makes heirloom plants so great? : old-fashioned
treasures to grow, eat, and admire / Judy Barrett ; art by
Victor Z. Martin.—1st ed.
      p. cm.—(W. L. Moody Jr. natural history series ; no. 41)
  Includes index.
  ISBN-13: 978–1–60344–219–0 (book/pb-flexibound : alk.
paper)
  ISBN-10: 1–60344–219–7 (book/pb-flexibound : alk.
paper)
  1. Gardening—Handbooks, manuals, etc.   2. Heirloom
varieties (Plants)—Handbooks, manuals, etc.   3. Low
maintenance gardening—Handbooks, manuals, etc.   4.
Cookery (Vegetables)   I. Title.   II. Series: W.L. Moody, Jr.,
natural history series ; no. 41.
SB453.B365   2010
635—dc22
2010016588

Contents

What Makes Heirloom Plants So Great?

What Is An Heirloom Plant?

*I*n many ways heirloom plants are just like heirlooms of any other kind. Whether it is a cut-glass bowl, a hand-made quilt, or a pickle crock that belonged to Grandma, an heirloom is something that has been used, enjoyed, treasured, and passed down from one generation to the next. Almost all the settlers who came to America, and then spread across the country in every direction, brought with them their favorite plants, whether in the form of seeds or bulbs or cuttings. Those plants have formed the basis of agriculture, gardens, and landscapes throughout the United States. If it weren't for heirloom plants, we'd be in an awful state!

But, of course, people are never satisfied. We also want sparkle-flecked purple plastic bowls from China, electric blankets with dual controls, and pickles packed by Vlasic™. In our enthusiasm for the new, we forget why the old was so good in the first place. Just so in the field of agriculture. Many new varieties of plants are introduced every year, all with real or imagined improvements: tomatoes with disease resistance, flowers with drought tolerance, field crops impervious to pesticides, and roses in previously unseen colors. The companies that sell seeds understandably want to sell as many as they can. They want to sell seeds to farmers who use a lot of seeds and want the latest varieties. So they drop the old varieties from their lists and replace them with newer ones that may or may not be better. And that is not necessarily a bad thing; it is just a different thing. The bad thing comes when the old varieties are lost and the home gardener, who has different standards for good plants, is left in the lurch.

In the gardening business *heirloom* is a flexible term and might mean a plant that has been around 50 years or more, or it might just mean a plant that's hard to find. For a while, heirloom roses were called "Antique Roses," but that designation has gradually changed to the common "antique and old garden roses" to include varieties that are not new but are not that old either. *Heirloom* is a nice catch-all phrase that fits antique and vintage alike. If it is sort of old and you love it, it's an heirloom.

Another characteristic of heirloom plants is that they propagate themselves directly from one generation to the next by producing seed that is viable without any human intervention. These are the natural hybrids we call "open-pollinated," which means they will self-fertilize or be fertilized by birds, insects, or the wind and produce delicious fruit or lovely flowers without human help. You can save the seeds of such plants and plant them year after year. There may be some natural variation, but you can control that if you want, and if not, your seeds may just get better naturally.

Hybrid plants are those that have been cross-pollinated: one variety of tomato has been crossed with another to create a tomato with characteristics of both the parents. Hybrids happen naturally all the time; there are few plants around today in the same form in which they originated millennia ago, because as the years passed, plants cross-pollinated and the healthiest crosses continued to propagate themselves.

In addition to natural hybridization, though, there is a lot of intentional hybridizing that goes on all the time at every level of horticulture—even in the home garden. Just selecting the best of your crop to save and propagate again next year is a way to hone the perfection of the seed and subsequent plant. In the giant agribusiness labs, however, hybridization takes on another form. The breeders there create what are known as F-1 hybrids. That means that the breeder takes a pure line of two different open-pollinated plants and cross-pollinates the two by hand. The resulting seeds will produce the desired plant—but only for that generation. The process has to be repeated each time that plant is grown. Such scientific breeding programs have made it possible not only to bring out the outstanding qualities of the parent plants, but also, in most cases, to enhance these qualities and add new characteristics to the resultant hybrid plants.

So the scientists cross two open-pollinated tomato plants, and the resulting fruit produces viable F-1 seed. Those are the seeds you buy in packages at the store. But if you cultivate the seeds from the tomatoes you grow, the new plants will not "breed true": they will not be like the plant you grew the first season. After the first generation, the F-1 plants produce seeds that are highly unreliable and can produce a bunch of different plants.

The most commonly offered commercial seeds and plants are F-1 hybrids. The first reason is simple: These hybrids can be patented and sold only by the creator of the cross. Creating the plants in the first place is expensive, but repeating the process and selling seeds and plants returns terrific profits. This is especially true when the hybrids are created for use in large quantities on farms—and that is the goal of most hybrid production.

The home garden market is very small compared with the commercial market, so hybrid programs are designed with the large grower in mind. They want fruits, vegetables, and ornamentals that will grow in a wide variety of climates, soils, and conditions. They want them to be uniform and predictable. In the case of food crops, they should keep well on the shelf, be machine harvestable, and transport easily. These are desirable characteristics for commercial growers, perhaps, but they are not features that home gardeners look for. In fact, home gardeners want almost completely opposite traits. We want plants that are well adapted to our specific climate and conditions. We want food that tastes terrific and would prefer that it not all ripen at the same time. Its shelf life is not too important, and the ability to ship it long distances is rarely a consideration. We enjoy picking by hand and don't have big machines to do that work. While large commercial growers want rows of plants that look just alike and produce all at the same time, we like diversity in size, shape, and bloom period.

On the other hand, there are some very good hybrids that we like in our garden. Alan Kapuler of Deep Diversity, a seed bank that preserves rare and valuable seeds, urges people to save seed from their favorite hybrids and grow them out until they are stabilized. This involves growing the seeds and seeing what comes up, saving seeds from the best of that generation, and repeating the process for several generations. It takes about three to five generations (or six to ten, depending on who you ask) to get a stable set of seeds from an original hybrid parent, but after that process you end up with an open-pollinated plant.

Heirloom plants that are not grown from seed can be propagated by taking cuttings or waiting for the plant to multiply. You sometimes see daylilies, garlic, irises, or daffodils growing in clumps along the roadside or in abandoned farmyards. These are the result of natural propagation; the bulbs (or tubers or corms) make new plants every year, and if you would like some of those plants in your garden, all you have to do is dig up some of the bulbs or corms or tubers and transplant them. Old roses, on the other hand, are best grown from cuttings. A snip here and there will provide you with a lovely rose garden.

Twenty years ago I moved from the city to the country and soon thereafter noticed big clumps growing in the ditches around my house. I realized they were garlic—an easy plant to identify by smell—and dug some up to plant in my yard. Just to be sure, I asked a neighbor about it and was told that it was "that old ditch garlic . . . unless of course it's death lily" (rural humor). At any rate, it turned out to be wonderful, mild, big fat rocambole garlic that has appeared in my garden and in my kitchen ever since. Easy to grow, easy to propagate, and delicious, this gift has gone with me when I moved and has gone to many friends' and relatives' gardens as well.

One way to characterize heirloom plants is to say that they grow without the aid or meddling of people. Old roses grow on their own roots and don't need grafting, old apples grow on old apple trees, old zinnias produce seeds that will even plant themselves if left to their own devices. That is, obviously, a little over-simplified, but the general idea is true. Heirloom plants are clearly much more self-sufficient than hybrids.

What Makes Heirlooms So Great?

Toughness and Adaptability

Perhaps one of the best things for the home gardener about growing heirloom plants is that these plants have a strong will to live. By their very nature, they are sturdy. Many antique roses have been found growing at abandoned farmhouses or in cemeteries, blooming happily without the benefit of a gardener. They would not have lasted all these years if they required intensive care. One of the reasons they have been around so long is that they can withstand conditions that will send lesser plants to the compost heap. Heirlooms have been around and seen it all—and developed the genetic where-withal to cope with it. They can survive too much water, not enough water, over-attentive gardeners, neglectful gardeners, diseases, and bugs. They may get a little ragged looking now and then, but they keep on going. And that is a great characteristic in a plant.

I know that in my experience I am an excellent gardener in March, April, and May, I slip a bit by June, and then in July and August I give up and go in the house with the air-conditioning. Nothing gets much attention until October, when the heat mitigates and I can enjoy being outdoors again. So I count on the plants to take care of themselves while I'm inside thinking about Canada or the Swiss Alps. Heirlooms are able to do that. They sort of hunker down and do what is necessary to stay alive. Some of them produce seeds to take care of the next season. Some die back a bit and send out really long roots to sustain themselves. But few just keel over at the arrival of one-hundred-degree days.

Those of us who garden organically also benefit from the toughness of heirlooms. They require little care and no chemicals. Of course we never really need those toxic products, but with heirlooms we aren't even tempted.

Naturally, heirlooms are not adapted to every location in the world. Old plants that do well in Nova Scotia probably won't thrive in Texas. You need to find the heirlooms that are appropriate to your growing conditions: soil, climate, and location. But many heirlooms travel well from one site to another with similar conditions. Many plants from China have immigrated to the United States and become standards in places with like conditions. The old China roses are heat-tolerant, disease-resistant, and a mainstay in gardens around the world. So when you are shopping through catalogs for new or old varieties to try, look to see where they are currently grown. If the climate is similar to yours, give them a try.

Easy Propagation

Related to their proven toughness is the ease of propagation of heirloom plants. Almost all heirloom vegetables grow from seed that can be saved from year to year. (Artichokes and asparagus are exceptions.) Most of these veggies were brought to America by our ancestors and have been passed down through the generations. Sharing seeds with neighbors, friends, or family members is a time-honored tradition, and this ability to pass along treasured plants is one factor that keeps them going.

To make the process even better, the longer a seed grows in a particular location, the better the plant gets in that location. All plants prefer one location over another. Some like deep, black soil; others prefer sandy, rocky soil. But heirlooms will adapt. Keep growing your seed in the same place and your crop with improve year after year.

Look at the Native Americans of New Mexico, who grow dryland gardens and have for many generations. When you visit those desert gardens, you are sure that absolutely nothing could grow there. The so-called soil is lumpy sand, rough and dry and unfriendly by all appearances. Yet those farmers know how to do it. They do not buy the latest corn seeds with new and improved genetic modifications. They plant the same corn that has been planted there for hundreds of years. And the corn produces every year. It doesn't pop up predictably two weeks after planting and grow as high as an elephant's eye. It waits until one of the infrequent rainfalls and then jumps up and grows like crazy. Healthy ears of corn are produced every season to feed the people and to provide enough for next year's seeds. Those corn kernels are specific to that place and produce well because they have adapted themselves to the conditions there.

The same can be accomplished in your garden, and you don't have to wait several generations to see the improvements. Many people who live in hot, dry climates have bought seeds from the nonprofit group Native Seeds/SEARCH. These are seeds grown by traditional groups throughout the Southwest and are all heirloom varieties. People who grow them in their home gardens find they adapt quickly and well to a bit more water than they were accustomed to in the desert.

A neighbor of mine went to visit his relatives in Germany and brought home an old German Chocolate tomato, both because it tasted great and because it was from the homeland. It has adapted beautifully to Central Texas and produces fine brown red tomatoes. Sadly, they don't actually taste like chocolate, but they do look sort of chocolaty and taste like great tomatoes.

The garlic I mentioned earlier migrated easily from the farm garden to the ditch without missing a beat. Lots of bulbs that produce beautiful flowers, such as lilies and daffodils, are thriving unattended in ditches, cemeteries, and other spots where they have settled themselves in nicely.

Roses and other plants that have to be propagated by cuttings are also easy. The traditional method of pinning a branch of a rambling rose to the soil until it sprouts roots couldn't be easier. Sticking a cutting into the ground under the mother bush or into a pot under a fruit jar is only slightly more trouble. Cuttings, like seeds, have been transported around the world and back. Scientists who try to trace the travels of, say, peppers from their origins in South and Central America end up with an amazing wandering path of migration. Plants have gone from their original source to pretty much everywhere else and back again. The reason is that old, un-messed-with plants are easy and adaptable and happy to see new sites.

There are several methods of propagating old plants. Which method you chose depends on the kind of plant involved.

DIVISION

Some plants create their offspring attached to the mother plant. Irises and other tubers, most bulbs such as daffodils and garlic, ferns, and many other plants can simply be divided, and you end up with multiple viable plants where there was originally only one. Plants that have a tendency to spread by runners are good candidates for division. Mints, verbena, ajuga, daisies, oregano, and others are inclined to ramble along and put down roots occasionally along the stem where it touches the ground. To determine if a plant can be divided, look at its roots. Are there multiple roots attached to multiple stems? If so, simply pull or cut the plants apart and replant them separately.

Division is the easiest way to propagate plants. Generally it is best to divide plants in the season opposite the one in which they bloom. For spring bloomers, divide in the fall; for fall bloomers, divide in the spring. That system allows a period for settling in and growth before the bloom season commences. It also protects the plant from the harshness of winter and summer by getting it established in the more temperate seasons.

CUTTINGS

When you take a cutting of a plant, you are creating a clone. Genetically, the plant that grows from a cutting is identical to the parent plant. Woody plants are especially good to take cuttings from. Many of them, even though they may produce seed, make better plants through cuttings than by seeding. Rosemary and lilac are good examples. Both are easy to propagate through cuttings, but both produce fairly small and unreliable seed.

To take a cutting, first find a plant that you really like. If you want a flowering plant, make sure the parent flowers. If you want a plant with berries, make sure the parent produces berries. Remember, your youngster will be genetically the same as the parent, and if the parent doesn't bloom, neither will the offspring. There is some variation in the type of wood you should cut. Some plants require soft wood cuttings; others, green or hard wood. If you're not sure, you can look up that specific plant or you can experiment. Generally, growth tips (the end of stems that are putting out new leaves) are your best bet for most cuttings.

Select a healthy tip and cut it 4–6 inches long (making sure one or two leaf nodes will be below soil level). Remove all of the leaves except the top two. Place in sand, potting soil, or any other well-drained mix and water regularly until new growth appears. Few plants like to be kept soggy, so it is essential that the medium drain well, but also, since the plant doesn't have roots yet, it needs a constant supply of moisture. Once new growth appears, you can assume you have roots and transplant your youngster to a bigger pot or into the ground.

You can take cuttings of almost anything with a stem: tomatoes, roses, geraniums, begonias, rosemary, artemisia, salvia and much more. Give the cuttings bright light but not direct afternoon sun and give them gentle feedings of seaweed or vitamin B1 to get those tiny hairlike roots growing quickly. Gradually move the young plants into the direct sun and let them get adapted to the heat before transplanting into the garden.

LAYERING

Mints and other running plants will stop and put down roots from time to time, giving you perfect new plants to move to another location. Other plants are agreeable to the principle involved but need some help accomplishing the deed. Roses, for example, can be forced to root along their stem in a process called layering. You first find a long, flexible cane and bend it gently to the ground. (Canes are the long, flexible stems of climbing or rambling roses.) Pin it to the ground some way—or put a rock on it to hold it down—with part of the cane on either side of the spot where it touches the ground. Then cover the place where it touches with soil and keep it moist. In a while you'll find that roots have grown into the soil. At that point, you can separate the growing tip from the original plant and transplant your young plant. Vines and other long, floppy-stemmed plants can often be layered to create new plants.

Air layering is used on plants that do not have flexible canes or stems. In this process a nick is made in the stem and held open with something like a wooden toothpick. The nick should go perhaps one-third of the way through the stem, but not all the way. The top of the plant needs to continue getting nourishment from the root. Around this wound wrap a bundle of moist potting soil, peat moss, coir, or other growing medium in a bandage of plastic wrap or other similar covering. Tape it together with masking tape, being careful to bundle up the growing medium but not cut off circulation from the stem. The bundle should be mostly airtight so the moisture won't evaporate. After a while you will see white roots growing through the soil in the plastic bandage. When you have a good little plastic-wrapped root ball, sever the new plant from the original plant, remove the plastic wrap, and plant your new baby either in a container or in the ground.

This method is often used on houseplants that get too tall for their spot. It serves the purpose of reducing the size of the old plant and creating a new one in the process. It is a little trickier than previously described methods, but it works, and it is fun when you succeed. If you fail, simply prune back the old plant and add the unrooted top to the compost pile.

SAVING SEEDS

Annuals are particularly good choices for saving seeds. Vegetables and annual flowers produce seeds readily, and saving them is not difficult. There are two standards for saving seeds. If you are saving seeds for your own use or to share with neighbors, you can relax and enjoy the process and save seeds to your heart's content, realizing that sometimes it won't work out as you planned. If you are saving seeds to sell or to offer through a seed exchange or seed bank, however, you have to be much more careful. In that case you owe it to the recipients of your seeds to thoroughly study the mechanics of sexual plant reproduction and ways to maintain purity of strains.

The principles of saving seeds are simple. You know that to make seeds grow you need light, warmth, and moisture. To save seeds, you need exactly the opposite: cool, dry darkness.

Saving Vegetable Seeds

Start small with a few varieties you want to save. Begin by clearly labeling your plants with stakes or tags to be sure you know what you have. If you want to be fairly sure of the purity of your seeds, plant only one variety of each type—one tomato variety, one pepper variety, one bean variety, one corn variety—to avoid cross-pollination. Otherwise you need to bone up on the distance required between different varieties to ensure purity (see appendix A).

To capture seeds, wait until they are fully mature. Leave them on the plant as long as possible (keeping in mind that rain or frost could damage them). Just before they are ready to break the pod or fall to the ground, pick the seeds and process them. Select seeds from several different fruits to get plenty of good old genetic diversity, making sure you select the best ones. Strength is born in diversity.

Beans, peas, and okra should all be left on the plant to dry until the seeds are fully mature and pods become brown. Don't wait, however, until they break open. Put the pods in the shade to dry thoroughly, and then remove the seeds.

Peppers are generally self-pollinating and don't cross easily. To be sure, however, leave some space between different varieties. Hot and sweet peppers will cross, with the hot predominating in the mix. Leave peppers on the plant until they become red. Cut the pepper pod in half and scrape the seeds onto paper and dry them thoroughly.

Cucumbers, squash, pumpkins, and melons all cross easily, so if you want to save seeds, grow only one variety of each. The fruit should be fully mature when it is picked. Scoop out the seeds and wash thoroughly to remove any pulp. Spread the seeds on newspaper or coffee filters to dry. Some recommend fermenting cucumber seeds as you do tomatoes.

Tomatoes are self-pollinating and don't cross easily. Allow the fruit to ripen thoroughly on the plant. Cut the tomato open and squeeze out the seeds into a small glass or plastic container of water. Let the mixture sit at room temperature for a couple of days. Seeds and pulp will ferment, and a white coating will form on top of the water. Add clean water to the mix to separate the clean seeds from the yuck. Clean, viable seeds will sink to the bottom of the container, allowing the floating seeds and pulp to be washed away. You can also simply pour the mess into a tea strainer and scrub any remaining pith away. Rinse thoroughly. Spread the seeds on a coffee filter to dry. Coffee filters are a good choice for drying damp seeds because the seeds don't stick to the filter, and the filter doesn't stick to the seeds.

Eggplant is ready to be harvested for saving the seeds when the fruit starts to get brown and shriveled. Split it open, remove the seeds, and wash them thoroughly to remove all pulp. Spread them out to dry quickly in a warm, bright spot, since damp eggplant seeds can germinate overnight.

Saving Flower Seeds

The principles for saving flower seeds are the same as for saving vegetable seeds. Wait until the flower seeds are completely ripe—when the flower is past its peak and at the point where you would normally deadhead it. Separate the seeds from the petals or pod and clean them as necessary. Few flower seeds are damp, so that makes saving them easier than saving vegetable seeds. Some seeds are encased in pods—butterfly weed, desert willow, yellow bells (esperanza), trumpet vine, and others have their own little seed cases that protect the seeds until they are mature. Take Nature's cue on these plants. Watch and wait until the pods turn brown and look as if they are just about to split open. You can capture the winged seeds of most plants like these if you pick them just as the pod is splitting. Remove the feathery substance designed to help the seeds disperse themselves and store the seeds in their papery husks.

The same is true of saving seeds from wild plants. Select your plant early in the season and then watch it. Just as the plant is about to drop its seeds, catch them. Don't ever take all the seeds from a wild plant. Take only a few and let nature spread the rest.

Saving Seeds of Trees and Shrubs

Once you have the idea about seed saving, the process is the same no matter the size of the plant. Pick the fruits when they are dead ripe. If the seeds are dry, all you have to do is save them. If they are moist, they should be dried. Wild or Mexican plums, for example, can be grown easily from seed. Wait until the fruit is ready to drop to the ground or has already dropped. Remove the pulp, wash the seeds, and dry them thoroughly. Plant in the spring and watch the tree grow.

The same is true of buckeye, redbud, vitex, and many other seed-producing trees and shrubs. Some plants, however, have specific requirements. The berries of many wild plants must pass through the digestive system of a bird or animal before they become viable seeds. If you consistently fail in germinating a native plant, that may be your problem.

STORING SEEDS

A vital first step in any seed saving project is to label your seeds. Throughout the process, keep the seeds labeled. Label the plants; label the seeds as soon as you separate them from the plants. Many seeds look a lot alike. All tomato seeds look pretty much the same whether they are for a huge yellow-fruited variety or a tiny red cherry. The same is true of other kinds of seeds, so label them immediately. As mentioned earlier, seeds need to be stored in a dark, cool, dry location. As soon as your seeds are dried, they should be put away safely. Do not ever bake your seeds. That will kill them. Also, avoid direct sunlight for the same reason. To test your seeds for proper dryness, give them the "break or bite" test. If a seed is too hard to bite or will break before bending, it's dry enough.

Containers should be airtight to keep out moisture. Glass jars are good storage containers for seeds, as are plastic bags with a tight seal. Be sure the seeds are completely dry when you put them away. Paper seed packages are obviously a good choice or all the commercial seed companies wouldn't use them. You can buy seed packets or use old envelopes or cheap envelopes from garage sales. Be sure you write all you know about the seeds on the envelope: the name of the plant, where you got it, what you've learned about it. Next season you'll be glad you did.

Many people like to put the seeds in the freezer for a couple of weeks to make sure any lingering bugs or larvae will be killed off. You can store the seeds in the freezer indefinitely if you are sure that no moisture can get into them.

There are many reasons to save seeds. Here is the short version:

1. When you find something you really love, you can be sure that you'll be able to grow it again and again.
2. Saving seeds allows you to share your treasures with friends and neighbors.
3. Saving seeds ensures that an old reliable plant is maintained for a longer period of time.
4. More and more commercial seeds are hybrids that are not reproducible by seed.
5. More and more commercial seed companies are limiting the number of varieties offered.
6. Commercial seeds are often treated with toxic chemicals.
7. Saving seeds maintains varieties related to the diverse cultures that settled this country.

8. Saving seeds allows for personal independence from commercial trends and economies.
9. Saved seeds are better adapted to your location, climate, and soil conditions.
10. Saving seeds helps maintain genetic diversity for the future.
11. You can invent your own varieties of plants by saving seeds.
12. You can protect varieties from genetic engineering by saving seeds.

There is some controversy about the safety of genetically modified organisms (GMOs). The push in modern plant breeding is toward GMO. Genetic engineering is striving for "the best" plant and narrowing choices as the process goes. The industry relies more and more heavily on genetic engineering to create seeds that are tolerant of pesticides and that have unusual characteristics. Some people refer to these as "Frankenseeds" or "Frankenfoods," pointing to the unpredictability of messing with Mother Nature. They say we simply don't know enough about these GMOs to rely on them completely for our food source.

Keep in mind that seeds have to be planted and grown. Unlike other antiques, you can't just store them away and keep them. So it is important to share them to keep the plant going. Seeds will become less and less viable as time goes by. They are living things that require growth to continue living.

One of my favorite garden books is *Passalong Plants* by Steve Bender and Felder Rushing (University of North Carolina Press, 2002). The whole book is based on the fact that heirloom plants are easy to propagate. It focuses on the old-fashioned plants that are easy to pass from one friend to another, from one garden to the next. In this process people make friends, acquire hardy and lovely plants, and keep old varieties going—and, they do this without spending a penny. What more could you ask?

Scent and Flavor

Having made the comment above about penny-pinching, I should say that, in my opinion we have become a nation much too motivated by dollars and cents. Everything is done with an eye to the bottom line. What's in it for me? Have I won the lottery yet? Forget everything else, follow the money. Well, heirloom plants give you a chance to consider some things that may be a bit more important than economic considerations. One of the reasons we've gotten into the current fix we're in now, of relying so heavily on F1 hybrids, is that many plant developers and sellers are always motivated by money. They want tomatoes that will travel across the country from field to market and still look like tomatoes. They want rectangular or square watermelons that will stack neatly on trucks and shelves. They want sweet peas that are vivid, neon colors and can take the heat. They want roses with two-foot-long stems and blossoms in deep purple.

The problem with the new and improved varieties is that in the transition from old to new often what is lost is what was great about the plant in the first place. What do you think of when you think of sweet peas? The scent, of course. White Shoulders perfume hasn't been a constant seller for generations because it has neon-colored bottles but because it smells like sweet peas. Sweet peas are tender and lovely flowers that prefer cool weather in which to grow and bloom. And they reward the gardeners who pay attention to their preferences with a heavenly fragrance that can sweeten a house in no time at all. They are called "sweet" peas after all, not gaudy peas.

And tomatoes? We've all tasted supermarket tomatoes. They bear a resemblance to pink, soft, watery Styrofoam. No taste. No texture. No gumption. Tomatoes that have traveled twenty-five hundred miles from field to market are not tomatoes. They are tomato-looking substances. And many of the new varieties, even locally grown, are not much better. But take a bite of a Cherokee Purple, feel the skin pop on a Yellow Pear, or slice up a German Johnson, and you know what "tomato" means. Tomato isn't just a look. It is a taste, a texture, an essence that cannot be faked. Heirloom varieties of tomatoes will out-taste any new tomato on the market. Sure, they won't ship as far, they are irregular in shape and size, and some are sometimes downright gnarly looking, but the taste is incomparable. Even people who don't like most tomatoes and 2-year-olds love heirloom tomatoes.

Almost all heirloom vegetable varieties have deeper, more complex, and more delightful flavors than their blander hybrid cousins. The hybrids are controlled by the seed companies. You can't save the seeds and have another generation of the same plant, so it is to their benefit that you have to buy their seeds every year. They also want to sell the same seeds to gardeners in Maine and in Texas and in Arizona and in California. So these seeds will not do really well anywhere, but they will do all right in almost every location. The fewer varieties they offer, the less trouble and the higher profit there is for them.

Now when I say this, I'm not talking about every seed company in the world or every plant breeder in the world. Mostly I'm talking about the big ones—the ones whose primary market is commercial growers (often the ones that are a subsidiary of the chemical companies that make lots of pesticides and herbicides). Fortunately, though, a growing number of small seed suppliers are focusing on saving and maintaining a supply of heirloom seeds, and I applaud them. They are listed in the back of this book. The problem is that those vegetables you buy at the store usually come from commercial growers who buy the standard seeds. And when you buy those veggies, you're missing so much flavor that it ought to be against the law.

If you grow your own or seek out farmer's markets where the farmers are adventurous and try different varieties, you'll be amazed at the difference in flavor—not only in tomatoes, but in all their produce. I thought carrots were carrots until I bought some old-fashioned carrots at the farmer's market. They were sweet and crunchy and fresh. You won't even have to bribe your kids with ranch dressing to get them to eat their vegetables if you offer them flavor-packed varieties.

Taste and scent are two good reasons to grow heirlooms. They are also purely personal reasons: you may love sweet peas and hate roses. I may prefer yellow tomatoes to purple. Given the large diversity among heirloom plants, you have lots of choices to grow the plants you really love, whether it is for their look, their taste, or their smell. Heirlooms are a mixed bag of colors, shapes, and habits. That's part of the fun.

Peculiarity

The element of weirdness in a plant should not be underestimated. This may not seem like a particularly good reason to choose a plant, but if it doesn't seem reasonable to you, you must not be an enthusiastic gardener. Most of the gardeners I know who really love to garden also love to find something peculiar to grow. We want something that no one else has or that isn't common around the neighborhood. We like unusual-looking vegetables, strange-tasting fruit, exotic blossoms, and more. I first grew many of my favorite garden plants simply as curiosities. Browse through any heirloom catalog and you'll find things you never heard of or saw before.

I can't imagine why anyone would grow the antique green rose except that it is odd. Here's what the Antique Rose Emporium in Texas has to say about this rose: "Every garden needs a conversation piece and the 'Green Rose' definitely fits that bill. This most rewarding rose is always in bloom. Granted the blooms may be hard to detect, but once you know what you are looking at, you'll find the bush is literally smothered. Perfect for floral arrangements or dried in bouquets, this rose lends its unique texture and contrasting color of green and bronze. Fragrance is spicy with a hint of pepper. You can expect continual bloom from this nicely rounded shrub throughout the season. A definite eye catcher!" This rose goes back to before 1845 and continues to be purchased, shared, grown, and enjoyed by a host of gardeners—and primarily for its peculiarity. "Conversation piece" is a kind way of saying "weird."

The same can be said for vegetables. The banana cantaloupe tastes delicious, but pretty much like a standard cantaloupe. Its appeal is in the shape. It is shaped like a banana and is yellowish like a banana. You can impress your friends with a cantaloupe that looks like a banana. Ho hum to cantaloupes that look like cantaloupes.

My first venture into garden writing was a book about tomatillos. Why? Because at that time tomatillos were unusual and weird. Nobody grew them; they were exotic heirloom exports from Mexico. So I got a couple of plants and put them in my garden. Lo and behold, they were excessively happy there. I had tomatillos coming out my ears. So I started trying to learn something about them and what to do with them and came up with very little. The upshot of the adventure was a book about growing and using tomatillos. They are very versatile and tasty, and it turns out you can do a lot with them. Today, tomatillos are as common as kiwi fruit, but they are still fun to grow and delicious to eat—and all because they were peculiar in the first place.

Biodiversity

Of all the reasons to grow heirloom plants, maintaining biodiversity may be the most important. It is also the reason I know the least about. I am not a scientific gardener and just squeaked by the required science courses I had to take in college. But I know that biodiversity is important for many reasons. The variety of life is what makes life interesting, persistent, and stable.

Biodiversity, short for biological diversity, means having a wide range of life in a place—whether the place is your garden or the whole world. It can apply to either plant or animal life, but we're talking about plant life here. Plant diversity means that there are a lot of different varieties with slightly different genetic makeup and habits. The genetic composition of a fruit or vegetable variety not only influences its appearance and flavor, but also affects characteristics such as the plant's ability to withstand extreme temperatures and resist pests and diseases.

Scientists who are managing the genetics of plants these days all begin with the original heirloom plants and work from there. Even if you are a fan of genetically modified plants, you will realize that having a broad base to work with is important. For example, when you grow the same variety of a crop across a wide area (big fields of corn, for example), you are creating a haven for pests and diseases that like that variety. In 1970 U.S. farmers lost one billion dollars after a disease killed uniform corn crops. Different varieties of the same plant have variation in their genetic makeup that makes them more or less resistant to disease and other problems. I've been told that if the Irish of the 1840s and '50s had grown many different varieties of potatoes, the blight that caused the famine then might not have been so devastating.

Even if you aren't interested in manipulating the genes of plants, a broad base is especially important. If you have a particularly hot summer, your chances of harvesting a good crop of beans depend on having some diversity in your garden. Some beans will be more heat-tolerant than others. Old varieties that have suffered through many summers will be more likely to produce beans than new varieties designed to produce in average temperature.

Pest control, pollination, productive soil, and resistance to disease are all dependent on a wide range of living things in the garden or on the farm. With industrial agriculture producing most of our food these days, and that industry's concentration on homogenizing and standardizing the crops it raises, we are losing diversity on a daily basis. It is falling to the small farmer and home gardener to keep varieties going that may be important in the future. Research on the healing properties of plants is ongoing, and new discoveries are always a possibility, but if the plant is lost before the research is done, we have lost something irreplaceable. We may need that genetic information in the future—to combat disease, to keep hunger at bay, to do things we can't even imagine today. Valuable genetic diversity cannot be recovered once it is lost.

According to the Food and Agriculture Organization of the United Nations, since 1900 approximately 75 percent of the world's genetic diversity of agricultural crops has been eliminated. In the past few decades mergers and consolidations have resulted in the creation of a few large agrichemical companies that control a huge percentage of the world's seeds. Their seeds are patented, controlled, and usually genetically modified. They must be bought from the company and cannot be shared. It is a scary prospect. Somehow a company that combines chemicals, drugs, and seeds for the food we eat is not reassuring.

So, while you grow heirloom varieties because they taste good, look good, and are a tad weird, remember that you are also doing an important service to your community and the world. Keep those plants going!

Stories

Collectors of art and antiques like to have a provenance on the pieces they buy—the story of their origins, their travels through time, the people and places associated with them. Heirloom plants have provenances as well. In my own garden are mementos of people I have known through the years. There is the rose that grew on the trellis on the back of my mother's house. I have a sedum from my favorite aunt's garden. There are irises that came from a very old and dear friend's mother's yard. I have tomatoes grown from seeds Malcolm Beck gave me years ago and that I have saved ever since. Porter tomatoes came from a neighbor. On a trip to Kentucky to get my first look at a new granddaughter, we stopped at a homestead by the side of the road selling pumpkins from their garden. I brought some home, and now a new generation is going strong in my garden. Looking into my yard is like browsing through a scrapbook. Every time I see those plants, I think of the people who shared them with me, and I smile. There are stories and memories there that go way beyond a pretty flower or tasty fruit.

And then there are plants not related to people I know but which have stories of their own: Roses associated with the Republic of Texas. Tomatoes carried by the Cherokees over years of trial and tribulation. Rue that is rumored to keep old boyfriends and other bad people away. Bee balm, the old symbol of rebels against English rule of America.

I can spend a happy and restful time reading through heirloom seed catalogs. Here is a sample from Seed Saver's Exchange: "Black Sea Man tomato—Small plants with medium-sized deep brown fruits, rich flavor. Looks incredibly odd when blanched and peeled, revealing skeleton-like veins under the skin." "Outhouse Hollyhock—Years ago, refined ladies just looked for the hollyhocks and didn't have to ask where the outhouse was." "Dancing or Spinning gourds—Children used to carry these gourds in their pockets to play with at school where they would spin them on their desks."

Heirloom plants all have stories, and their stories are fascinating, delightful, sad, and happy by turn. The ancient tales of the use of herbs in battle, in mysteries and magic, and in a myriad of ways are a great part of the joy and pleasure of growing and using those old plants. Gardeners love to learn about plants and enjoy the stories that go with them. You can imagine what led to the naming of these vegetables: Mortgage Lifter tomatoes, Dragon's Tongue green beans, and Tom Thumb popcorn. Other varieties make you want to know more: Susan's Red Bibb lettuce—Who was Susan anyway? Canoe Creek Colossal melon—Where is Canoe Creek and why are their melons so big? Jack-in-Prison—There's a story there!

Personal Favorites: Food

Tomatoes

Like almost every other gardener in the world, I eagerly await the first tomatoes of the season. The traditional breakfast BLT sandwich starts off the tomato season at our house. You cannot compare the taste of a homegrown tomato with any product you find on the grocer's shelf. That fact is commemorated in the song by Guy Clark: "Homegrown tomatoes. Homegrown tomatoes / What'd life be without homegrown tomatoes?"

As cheerful as the song is, it isn't completely true. You can buy home-grown tomatoes if you rush down to the farmer's market and get in line early. Particularly at the beginning of the season, the longing for fresh tomatoes is so strong that otherwise civilized people will push, shove, and speak unkind words to get closer to the farmer selling homegrown tomatoes.

Tomatoes are native American plants that originated somewhere in Central America. As early as 500 BC, people in Southern Mexico were cultivating tomatoes. The Aztecs grew them in their gardens around AD 700. Those early tomatoes were probably small and yellow, but they were tasty, and the early Americans had enough sense to know that. Not so the Europeans, who took some home as attractive ornamental plants. In the 1500s Europeans got a glimpse of this tasty fruit and were scared. In many places it was thought to be poisonous. The Italians called it "golden apple" and the French "love apple." Those French are always optimistic when the possibility of a plant's being an aphrodisiac is concerned.

Some sources say that the reason tomatoes were thought to be poisonous was that the elite of Europe ate from pewter dishes high in lead content. The acidity of the tomatoes released the lead, and lead poisoning resulted. Poor folks didn't have that problem since they didn't have pewter, so they were quicker to incorporate tomatoes into their diets. Not surprisingly, Italy was one of the first countries in Europe to develop a taste for tomatoes. They are still a staple in Italian cuisine. As explorers traveled around the world, they took tomatoes with them, along with other exotic crops.

By the mid-1800s everyone was growing and enjoying tomatoes, particularly those in southern regions with longer growing seasons. The most common tomatoes are red, but heirloom varieties are available that produce pink, orange, purple, black, green, white, and yellow fruit. They range in size from the tiny currant and wild cherry types to huge slicers. Home gardeners have the luxury of growing several different types and combining them in the kitchen to create beautiful and tasty dishes.

But tomatoes aren't only pretty and delicious; they are good for you, too. They are high in lycopene, an antioxidant, and are also high in vitamin C plus good amounts of vitamin A, vitamin K, vitamin B6, folate, potassium, manganese, iron, magnesium, phosphorus, and other minerals. As a source of fiber, one medium tomato equals one slice of whole wheat bread and contains only 35 calories.

I like to grow several different types of tomatoes each year. For one reason, each year is a little different, and the tomato that did best last year might not be the one that does best this year. For another, I like the variety of taste and color that combine to make a dish that is greater than the sum of its parts. Mixing yellow and red and purple tomatoes together looks great and is fun, too—not to mention the added benefit of impressing your friends.

One of my favorite old tomatoes is called Italian Rose. One problem with heirlooms is that they have very flexible names. Everyone who grows them is likely to call them by a different name, and in some cases nobody knows their real name. I've seen some tomatoes in seed catalogs that sound like this tomato and may be the same, but I'm not sure. I got the seeds for this tomato from Malcolm Beck, founder of Garden-Ville Products in San Antonio, about fifteen years ago. He had gotten it from Howard Garrett, garden writer and personality in Dallas, a few years before that. I don't know where Howard got it. Malcolm grew it and liked it and saved the seeds. He shared some with me, and I started growing it as well. It is a big slicing tomato that is a pinkish red color. It sometimes has deep ribs around the stem end and on occasion looks a little gnarly, but generally it is pretty and it tastes terrific. It has a full-bodied flavor and is perfect for eating fresh off the vine or sliced with basil and mozzarella. I like big tomatoes because they look so lush and generous.

I saved the seeds, as did Malcolm, for a few years, and then I shared them with my friends Sam and Cathy Slaughter, who run a wholesale nursery, Gabriel Valley Farms, in Jonah, Texas. They grew the tomatoes for me and offered some to their customers as well. The tomatoes were very popular, and I hope that many of the people who bought plants from the Slaughters also saved the seeds.

We almost lost this terrific tomato one year, though—an example of how fragile heirloom varieties can be. Malcolm, who knows better, left his seeds in an open bowl on a shelf, and the mice ate them all. Another year, the guys at the nursery mixed up the labels, and the seedlings with the Italian Rose label were not Italian Rose at all. It is easy for such a treasure to slip away. That's why I always encourage people to save some seeds. Tomato seeds last at least five years, so you don't have to plant them every single year, but it is nice to see how they evolve in your garden and how well they produce. There is no way for me to know who else is growing this tomato or even what they are calling it, but I hope it keeps going for a long time. It is a terrific tasty treat that I certainly want in my garden for a long time.

Another favorite of mine and of many other gardeners is the Cherokee Purple. A deep red purple fruit and distinctive flavor make this one of the most popular and most widely available of the heirloom varieties. Reputed to have come from the Cherokee people in Tennessee, the Cherokee Purple is dark and mysterious looking, and the flavor is out of this world. Purple tomatoes seem to have a tang and complexity that many other tomatoes don't have. It is hard to describe taste, and if you aren't careful you end up sounding like a wine connoisseur—"a perky little tomato with a sense of itself and a flip on the end," or something like that. At any rate, most people agree that Cherokee Purple is a great-tasting tomato. I've grown it in the ground and in containers, and it is a reliable producer.

Young Cherokee Purple fruit is green all over, then the body of the tomato begins to take on a dusky red color and the top or shoulders remain green. When it is fully ripe, the green fades and the purple and red take over. Inside, the juice is deep red and gorgeous. Luckily, this tomato is readily available through catalogs and more and more often at your local nursery. The plant, like most heirloom varieties, grows tall and needs support in the form of a cage or other contraption to hold the limbs and fruit off the ground. The indeterminate form that is common among heirlooms means that the plant will keep growing rather than reaching a terminal and tidy height that many hybrid plants are programmed for. My heirlooms typically reach the top of my five-foot-tall cages, and then grow upward for a while before cascading down as if they were in a hanging basket.

My favorite big yellow tomato is called Persimmon because it looks like a persimmon, of course. Another beefsteak-style tomato, this one is yellow tending toward orange and tastes robust and flavorful. I used to be prejudiced against yellow tomatoes, primarily because I once made yellow tomato salsa, and the result reminded me too much of my days as a young mother changing diapers. But if I stay away from salsa, I find this tomato just about perfect. The individual fruits can weigh as much as a pound each and are smooth and beautiful as well as tasty. Dating from the 1880s, this tomato has proven to be productive and sturdy in my garden.

Yellow tomatoes are said to be lower in acid than others, and maybe that is why they are often sweet and tasty. One of the oldest tomatoes in cultivation is the Yellow Pear. Grown since the 1800s, this small, pear-shaped tomato is low in acid with a sweet flavor. It is delicious in salads, pickled, or in jams, but it is also the sort of tomato that rarely makes it into the house because the gardener and the gardener's relatives are inclined to pop the fruit into their mouths before they get inside.

Yellow Pear, which is somewhat more vigorous than its Red Pear cousin, will continue to set fruit until frost. Although big tomatoes are yummy and impressive, it is the smaller varieties that will keep on going when the heat becomes oppressive. It is said that tomatoes will not set fruit once the temperature hits 90–95 degrees F, but that isn't always true. Smaller heirlooms will just keep going and going.

The Porter tomato, which was developed in Stephenville, Texas, by the now-closed Porter Seed Company, is a fine example of that. During a recent summer when we had in excess of 100-degree days for two months straight, my Porter tomato plant kept on setting fruit and producing lovely and tasty egg-sized and egg-shaped tomatoes. As the heat persisted, the tomatoes got a little smaller, but that was the only indication that the plant was stressed. I had tomatoes all summer from that one plant. Matt's Wild Cherry, one of the closest we have to the original tiny tomato plants, will also continue to produce no matter how hot it gets. These very small tomatoes are a burst of sweetness in your mouth when you bite into them—almost like candy!

Picking heirloom tomatoes is as much fun as picking out a new summer shirt. There are so many choices: red, green, white, yellow, purple, orange, and striped combinations. Personally I have never taken to the white and green varieties (I can't tell when they are ripe), but it is all a matter of personal taste, and it is a delightful process finding out which are your favorites. There is no such thing as a bad heirloom tomato fresh from the garden.

No matter which heirloom tomato you decide to grow—and it is fun to try at least one each year that you haven't tried before—follow the basic rules of tomato growing. The most important rule is to get them in the ground as early as you can. If you buy small plants before it is time to put them in the garden, move them up to gallon pots and let them grow in a sunny spot, bringing them indoors when the weather gets too cold. Tomatoes need full sun for their entire growing season. Once frost is done, put them into a bed or container that has been enriched with compost. A handful of colloidal clay (rock phosphate) under the roots will help your young plants get off to a rapid start. Feed them with fish emulsion and seaweed at least every two weeks. I like to put my tomatoes in a cage as soon as they are in the ground and wrap that cage with row cover fabric, top to bottom. The fabric will protect the young plants from cold nights and, more importantly, from harsh spring winds that can dry them out in no time. It doesn't block water or sunshine.

Be sure to water regularly, and as the tomato plant grows, put a layer of mulch around the base to keep away weeds, keep the soil temperature steady, and keep the soil moisture near the roots. Mulching with compost will provide continuous nutrients to the plants as well as doing duty as mulch. Remove the cloth when the plant reaches the top of the cage. If it starts blooming before then, remove the cover from the top of the cage and shake the cage gently when you walk by. That will encourage pollination from the top of the plant down to the bottom.

In my opinion, a ripe tomato is a work of art in itself and can't be improved on with a lot of fancy footwork in the kitchen. Mostly, I eat tomatoes raw—sliced, on sandwiches (BLT for breakfast), in salads, chopped up in cottage cheese, combined with onions, basil, mozzarella, avocado, and whatever else is fresh. Still, there is one recipe that I love and that my family waits for each summer.

Fresh Tomato Spaghetti

Chop up a variety of fresh, ripe tomatoes of as many colors as you have. Four cups is a good amount if you are feeding four to six people.

Add 1 medium onion, diced small
1–2 cloves of garlic, diced small
1 lb. mozzarella cheese, diced small
Small handful of fresh basil, sliced
Smaller handful of fresh oregano, chopped
Drizzle of unflavored rice vinegar
Healthier drizzle of olive oil
Salt and freshly ground pepper

Mix and let sit at room temperature for an hour or so before serving over hot cooked spaghetti. Sprinkle parmesan over the top.

This is a very flexible recipe. You can change the cheese if you like. I've used cheddar, muenster, feta, and whatever else was in the fridge. You can also add fresh peppers from the garden or cucumbers or parsley. Vary vinegars, using white wine, red wine, or balsamic to change the taste. Adjust the flavors to suit yourself and your fellow diners. It is a beautiful dish and showcases the fabulous flavors and colors of heirloom tomatoes.

Squash

I have to admit that squash is not my favorite vegetable. I never tasted squash growing up, so I assume it wasn't my mother's favorite either. Cooked squash often is too seedy, too mushy, and too bland. Raw squash is all those, except mushy, and sometimes it is spongy.

Still, squash is one of the mainstays of the hot summer garden, and my husband loves it, so I started looking for my favorite variety. The word *squash* comes from the Massachusetts Indian word *askutasquash*, which means "eaten raw." There are three basic groups of squash: winter squash (*Cucurbita maxima* and *C. moschata*), summer squash (*C. pepo*), and pumpkin (*C. maxima*). They are botanically all simply squash, but the division makes it simpler to talk about the different types. All of the squashes are native American plants and were cultivated early on by native people.

Known among North American natives as one of the three sacred sisters—corn, beans, squash—the plants were an important source of food for most tribes. Long before Columbus laid eyes on North America, the Native Americans had learned to cultivate summer squashes and pumpkins. We all remember the story of Squanto teaching the first settlers how to grow corn and squash, crops never before seen by Europeans. That generosity saved many a Pilgrim's life and led to the tradition of pumpkin pie for Thanksgiving dinner.

Remnants of old seeds found in caves in Ecuador have been proven to be more than ten thousand years old, older than any other known cultivated plant. Wild squash was thought to be easy to find and to provide good nutrition for hunter/gatherers and to grow easily when planted. Thus perhaps it was the squash that marked the beginning of agriculture as we know it. Corn wasn't cultivated for another two thousand years.

All parts of the squash are useful. The seeds, flowers, and fruit are edible, and the hard shells of gourds, members of the squash family, serve as vessels. Winter squash keeps well after the growing season is over without any effort. And, of course, saving seeds for the next season is easy—just don't eat them all.

Although the squashes originated in Central America and Mexico, they traveled north to what is now the United States and then to Europe

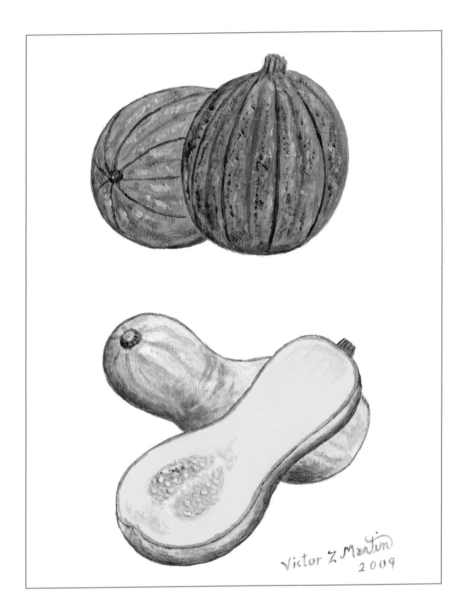

Victor Z Martin
2009

when the Spanish conquistadores returned home. Because they like relatively long, hot summers, squashes are not widely grown in colder areas of Europe and Canada. When Agatha Christie's fictional detective Hercule Poirot retired to grow "marrows," he was experimenting with that exotic vegetable from faraway lands: squash.

Other English authors have also found squash of interest. Louisa May Alcott, in *Little Women,* created this little tale-within-a-tale:

Once upon a time a farmer planted a little seed in his garden, and after a while it sprouted and became a vine and bore many squashes. One day in October, when they were ripe, he picked one and took it to market. A grocerman bought and put it in his shop. That same morning, a little girl in a brown hat and blue dress, with a round face and snub nose, went and bought it for her mother. She lugged it home, cut it up, and boiled it in the big pot, mashed some of it with salt and butter, for dinner. And to the rest she added a pint of milk, two eggs, four spoons of sugar, nutmeg, and some crackers, put it in a deep dish, and baked it till it was brown and nice, and next day it was eaten by a family named March.

I much prefer winter squash to summer squash. Winter squash has deeper colors and more taste, in my opinion. Probably butternut is my favorite because it is lovely and easy simply to cut in half and bake. The idea that you need to add sugar to winter squash is silly. It is naturally sweet, and the addition of a little salt and some cinnamon is all that is necessary. Butter is good, too, but adding sugar, unless you are making a pie, is unnecessary.

Tatume is an interesting squash variety. A native of Mexico, it is very heat and drought tolerant and produces what we think of as both summer and winter squash. If you harvest the green globes when they are about the size of baseballs, they are delicious used as summer squash. If you let them continue to grow and ripen until the skin is golden, they have a deeper flavor more like that of winter squash. For some reason squash bugs don't like this variety very well, so that's another good reason to grow it.

Actually, most of the winter squashes can be eaten before they reach maturity—thereby becoming summer squashes. The seasonality here deals with when you eat them, not when they grow. Summer squash has to be eaten soon after it is picked, or it spoils. Winter squash can be kept for a long time and eaten well after harvest.

After some experimentation I found a summer squash that I love.

It is an Italian heirloom variety that goes by several names. I get my seeds from Renee's Garden Seeds, and she calls this squash Trombetta di Albenga. The seed packet says, "This wonderful Italian heirloom summer squash is a vigorous climbing vine, producing many 12 to 15 inch, lime green fruits with a curvaceous trombone shape and a delicate mild taste with a hint of nutty artichoke flavor."

One of the things I like best about this squash is that the skin is thin, and when the fruit is young there is no need to peel it. The inside is firm and seedless, and it actually has a good taste without the addition of cheese or tomatoes or onions or all the other things I have to add to yellow squash to make it taste good. It is also a beautiful plant. The big heart-shaped leaves have silvery skeleton decorations, and of course the big yellow flowers are lovely. The squash itself hangs down on the vine and looks sort of like Christmas decorations. It will quickly cover a fence, trellis, or other structure you plant it near, creating a beautiful background of greenery.

You can use this squash in any recipe that calls for winter or summer squash, and you can also use it to make bread-and-butter pickles just as you would cucumbers. Pick it when the fruit is 10–12 inches long. A type of zucchini, this squash doesn't get watery or mushy when lightly cooked, but it does produce generous amounts of fruit. And one of these big squashes will go a long way, so get ready to share with the neighbors.

All squash have the same growing requirements. They should be planted in rich soil in full sun as soon as the soil has warmed. Plant the seeds in groups of three or four together in a hill of soil about 1 inch deep and 4 inches from vertical support. Thin to the strongest seedling from each hill or to 12 inches apart along a fence. Water and fertilize often to keep the plants growing quickly. Squash bugs and squash vine borers are the bane of squash gardeners. The Trombetta usually grows so vigorously that it can survive a borer attack, but keep a close eye on your young plants and pick off any bugs you see. Plants well fed and watered will be less susceptible to pests.

Most squash grow on long, vining plants, but there are some bush varieties. These can be grown closer together and stand on their own stems. Like all annual vegetables, squash are heavy feeders and should be given some organic fertilizer on a regular basis. A mulch of compost is always a good idea, but any other mulch will be fine, too.

There are many heirloom squash choices. Look through a catalog and you'll want to grow them all. Experiment with different kinds each year. Check the list in the back of the book to see which will cross-pollinate. Remember, you don't have to grow everything you eat. Visit your local farmer's market to see what others are growing and give them a try.

Small farmers love to see which varieties appeal to their customers and pick ones they themselves enjoy.

Here's a good recipe that will work with whatever kind of squash you have.

Stuffed Squash

2 large squashes
2 Tbsp. oil
1 cup chopped onions
1 cup chopped, peeled, and seeded tomatoes
1 cup cooked rice
¼ cup pine nuts
½ cup chopped parsley
1 Tbsp. chopped fresh mint
Salt and pepper to taste
Marinara, tomato, or spaghetti sauce

Cut the squash in half lengthwise (it may not be easy). Scoop out the seeds and steam the squash over boiling water until the meat is fork tender but the skin is firm.

Heat oil over medium heat. Add onions and cook until tender.

Add pine nuts and cook for a few more minutes. Add rest of ingredients including chopped squash scooped out of shell, except for sauce and heat through, stirring well.

Stuff squash with rice mixture. Place in shallow baking dish and add about ¼ inch of water to the bottom of the pan. Cover with foil and bake in a preheated 400°F oven for 30 minutes.

Serve with your favorite marinara sauce or homemade tomato sauce. Serves 4.

This is a great thing to do with those old squashes that hide under the leaves until they get too big. You can also use it with the large Trombetta squash, and it works with winter or summer varieties. It is a great entrée for lunch or dinner.

Gourds

Strictly speaking, gourds are a member of the squash group, but this isn't a strictly-speaking sort of book, so we'll talk about them separately.

The best thing about gourds is that they are fun. They are goofy-looking things that come in all sizes and shapes. They are warty and slick and apple-shaped and long and skinny and short and fat and colored with every gaudy shade in the crayon box. Although gourds have many traditional and somber uses, I'm sure that their main purpose in the garden world is to be entertaining.

One gourd, known as Cave Man's Club or Dinosaur, has crumpled, dark green skin and is shaped as you might expect. Speckled Swan gourds are light green with white splotches and graceful necks, heads, and beaks that look like those of swans. The Bule gourd is a French heirloom shaped like a large apple but covered with what Baker Creek Heirloom Seeds calls "attractive warts." Somehow "attractive" and "warts" don't automatically go together in my mind, but on a gourd they are right.

As vegetable clowns, gourds are fun to grow and fun to look at. If you have never gone to a gourd show, you should make a point of doing so. It is amazing what people can do with these dried shells. I've

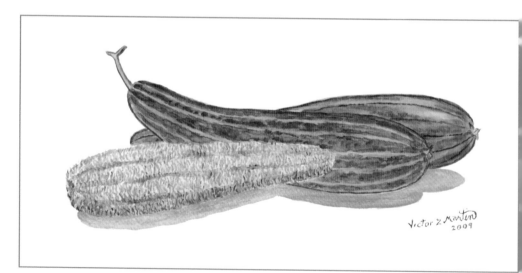

seen tables made of long-necked gourds, hats made of gourds, a zillion Santa Clauses and bird houses. They've been used to make lamps, sets of dishes, rattles, and anything else an imaginative person can create. It is such a pleasure to see how people can take a humble crop and turn it into a work of art—or at least a work of humor.

Gourds are very old plants and were domesticated early on in the history of mankind. Generally gourds are of the Lagenaria family, but some are regular old *Cucurbita pepo,* the same classification as summer squash. The distinctive characteristic of gourds is that their shells become very hard when they are mature. It is this hardness that makes them impervious to water and other substances, and that is what makes them so useful.

For centuries people have been using gourds for one purpose or another. Before the invention of pottery, gourds were used to hold water, grain, seeds, and anything else that needed holding. Shaped into bowls or bottles, the gourds were often decorated and cared for as essential household objects. Dipper gourds have long handles that are just right for dipping and serving water or food. The first pieces of pottery were made to mimic the size and shape of useful gourds.

Gourds are also used as resonating chambers on certain musical instruments. Both stringed instruments and drums have been made from rounded gourds. Birdhouse gourds are home to many species of birds, particularly the purple martin, a friend to farmers and gardeners alike. The dancing or spinning gourd, mentioned earlier, was once a favorite childhood toy that spun like a top when placed on a hard surface.

According to Wikipedia (and everyone who quotes Wikipedia), there is archeological evidence that gourd skins were used to replace missing parts of the skull during Neolithic times. (I shudder to think!) The hard skin of a gourd was placed over the skull under the skin to cover a hole left by crude surgery with stone tools.

Some young gourds are also edible. Picked small and green, the loofah gourd, the Italian heirloom Serpente di Sicilia, and the Thai Bottle gourd are said to taste delicious when they are cooked.

I am particularly fond of the loofah gourd. There are several different varieties; some are called loofah, some are called sponge gourds, others are called dishrag gourds, and some are called angled gourds. What they have in common is that when the gourd is dry and the outer shell is removed, the fiber inside serves as a scrubber—of bodies, pots and pans, dishes, and anything else that needs scrubbing. The fiber is gentle enough to be a good exfoliant on human skin and tough enough to use to wash the car. You can buy loofahs at snooty beauty supply and gift shops, or you can grow your own. Inside the fiber scrubber are lots of black seeds just waiting to be planted. (Take them out before scrubbing, whether you plan to plant them or not.)

Loofahs grow on a long, fast-growing vine that makes a perfect cover for a fence, trellis, side of a barn, or anything else where you have space for a vine to climb. The flowers are white or yellow depending on the type you grow, and they look pretty when they bloom. Then come the light green gourds, which are sort of long and oval-shaped. Some varieties (that Italian variety, for example) are really long and skinny and look something like snakes.

Left on the vine to mature, the loofah will become light brown and the outside will be brittle. You can leave the plant alone until frost kills the vine and then harvest the gourds, or you can pick the gourds as they become ripe and let them finish drying in a shady, breezy, dry location. Remove the shell and the seeds, and your loofah can be cut into sections with household scissors if it is very long.

Loofahs are great plants for kids to grow. They are easy to plant, grow quickly, and are showy, and the kids can participate in the entire process—eat a few when they are little, water and fertilize them as they grow, then harvest, peel, and scrub.

Grow gourds as you would squash: with lots of sun, water, and fertilizer. Grow them on a support if you can, because the vines grow very long (15–20 feet) and will take up a lot of space on the ground. For big gourds like the bushel basket, you'll have to give them ground space, because the fruit is too big and heavy to hang from a suspended vine.

Pumpkins

Yet more squashes! For many years I didn't grow pumpkins because I was afraid they would take up too much room. Then one year I planted a few spooky white Casper pumpkins and was amazed at how well they did. Somehow I expected that it was too hot to grow pumpkins in Texas. After all, the pictures I've seen show some lovely New England pumpkin patch with blazing fall colors in the background and people wearing sweaters. In my garden it was hotter than hot, but the pumpkins were going strong. They piddled around growing vines and male flowers for a couple of months, then whoa! All of a sudden I had white pumpkins all over the place. Although they were planted in raised beds, the vines jumped the borders and took off across the back yard. That was okay with me. Big green leaves looked lots better than my tired grass. And the pumpkins were both beautiful and tasty. I gave my grandkids some to carve for Halloween, cooked and froze some, and donated the rest to the local food bank. Everybody had pumpkin pie that year.

Then I moved from the country to town, where there was no room for those long, wandering vines, I thought. But I still had a soft spot in my heart for pumpkins, and what is autumn without a pumpkin or two? On the way home from a trip to Kentucky to see my new baby grand-daughter, we came upon a roadside pumpkin stand. The lady selling the pumpkins also grew them in her backyard, and they were lovely. She was a member of a religious community that believed in self-sufficiency and so sensibly grew only heirloom varieties of which she could save seed. I bought several and brought them home for decorations and for cook-ing. One of my favorites was a flat, cheese-shaped pumpkin with a pale salmon color. It was medium-small sized and smooth and pretty. I put the pumpkins on the front porch and enjoyed them until it was time to replace them with Christmas decorations.

By then, given our hot fall weather, they were looking a little sad, so instead of trying to cook the remaining pale pumpkin, I decided it was mulch. As far as I am concerned, anything that is made of organic mate-rial is potential mulch: pecan shells, corn shucks, coffee grounds, pump-kins. So I tossed the pumpkins off the side of the porch into a flower bed and forgot about them. Now this flower bed is on the side of the house

where I rarely go. I had planted some old roses in the bed and some orange cosmos, which reseed every year and completely fill up the bed, covering the roses and anything else that might be there. So imagine my surprise the next spring when I saw large leaves creeping out from under the cosmos and a vine making its way out of the flower bed into the yard.

I didn't know what it was, but I'm always happy when something volunteers and grows enthusiastically (like the cosmos), so I left the vine alone. After a while it was heading toward the neighbor's driveway, so I picked it up and moved it to the edge of the bed and let it follow the border around toward the front of the house. Pretty soon I saw big yellow flowers, which were followed by lovely little pale pumpkins. We got about seven pumpkins off that volunteer vine, and they were all nice and salmon-colored and firm and lovely. That pumpkin loved me as much as I loved it. It sprouted in the shade where it wasn't supposed to grow and grew for several feet under the dense cover of other plants. It was never fertilized and rarely watered. All of the rules of pumpkin growing were broken, and it still produced beautiful fruit. I was so proud!

Once again the kids got jack-o'-lanterns and I decorated. We had a new grandbaby then, so she got puréed pumpkin, which was very good for her. We had pie and pumpkin bread and mashed pumpkin at the Christmas brunch. And I still had a couple of pumpkins left over after the holidays. I cut one open and carefully saved the seeds before cooking it. The other I left on the bottom shelf of an open cabinet in the kitchen. About the end of February I noticed that the pumpkin on the shelf was beginning to ooze. I hadn't been paying attention, and it was rotting through the bottom. I took it out and threw it into the back flower bed farthest from the house—more mulch. When spring began to whisper, I got out my saved pumpkin seeds and planted them in 4-inch pots that I'd saved from last year as well. The seeds came up, and I had healthy little plants to put into the garden and share with some friends. And, of course, you guessed it. My mulch pumpkin came up like gangbusters. When the plants I had carefully nurtured just the right way were about a foot long, the "mulch" was already setting fruit. I had two pumpkins ripe by the end of June, when the other ones were just getting started.

So there you go. Heirlooms are not only sturdy, tough, and easy to propagate; they are a little headstrong as well. My conclusion is that the best way to plant pumpkins is to throw one onto the ground and forget about it. There are plenty of seeds in there, and if you don't disturb its resting place, some of them are bound to come in contact with the soil and germinate. This probably wouldn't work in climates where the weather is very cold, but then again, it might. One of the lessons I learned long ago is that the gardener is rarely as much in charge as she thinks she is. Plants, like people, can be willful and perverse when survival is at stake. If I don't plant my pumpkins at the right time, they will just plant themselves.

On the other hand, there is another good reason to go to the trouble of saving pumpkin seeds. According to some sources, pumpkin seeds are one of nature's almost perfect foods. They are a natural source of beneficial constituents such as carbohydrates, amino acids, and unsaturated fatty acids. They contain most of the B vitamins and niacin, along with vitamins C, D, E, and K. They also have the minerals calcium, magnesium, potassium, and phosphorus. To preserve as many nutrients as possible, roast seeds at 150 degrees F. Combine seeds with salt and butter or oil and cook on a baking sheet until light brown, about 20 minutes, stirring occasionally. Raw pumpkin seeds have been used to treat bladder and prostate problems, and in folk medicine they are credited with curing kidney problems and eliminating parasites from the intestines. So when you save your pumpkin seeds, put some aside to eat. Store them in the fridge to keep the oil from becoming rancid.

One of my favorite ways to use pumpkin is in sweet bread. These loaves can be baked then frozen and taken out whenever a treat is needed. My mother-in-law used to bake pumpkin bread in one-pound coffee cans. She'd take the cylinders of baked bread from the cans, wrap them in plastic wrap with a cheery bow on top, and then give the nice little cylinders as holiday gifts.

Cook your pumpkin by cutting it in half or in quarters if it is large and removing the seeds to clean and save. Put the pumpkin on a baking dish, cover with foil, and bake in the oven at 350 degrees F until it is soft. Cooking time will depend on the size of the pumpkin, but it will probably be thirty minutes to an hour. Remove the skin and mash the pumpkin. Remove any stringy part that remains near the center. It you want it really smooth (for baby, for example), run it through the blender or food processor.

Pumpkin Bread

2 cups all-purpose flour
1¼ cups brown sugar, firmly packed
1 cup granulated sugar
1 cup chopped pecans
½ cup raisins
1½ tsp. baking soda
1½ tsp. ground cinnamon
1¼ tsp. ground nutmeg
¾ tsp. salt
¾ tsp. ground cloves
½ tsp. ground allspice
½ tsp. ground ginger
(You can substitute 2 tsp. pumpkin pie spice for all the spices.)
3 large eggs
1¾ cups mashed pumpkin
¾ cup vegetable oil

Preheat oven to 350°F. In a large bowl, mix all the dry ingredients
   until they are well blended.
In another bowl, whisk together eggs, pumpkin, and oil until well
   blended.
Add wet ingredients to flour mixture and stir just until well
   blended. Pour equally into two oiled 8½ × 4½–inch loaf pans
   (with 2⅔ cups capacity each).
Bake until bread pulls away from the sides of the pans and a
   wooden toothpick inserted in the center comes out clean, about
   50 to 60 minutes. Let bread cool in pans on a rack for about 15
   minutes. Cut around outside edges of bread and invert onto
   racks. Cool thoroughly.

Cucumbers

There is something about cucumbers that says "fresh." Probably it is because they are made up mostly of water and we usually eat them cold, but their crunch and mild flavor help too. They taste like a bright spring day with still a little nip in the air. The phrase "cool as a cucumber" confirms what everyone thinks of this refreshing, delightful fruit. After all, what other vegetable can you put over your eyes to calm and soothe a tired brow?

Cucumbers originated in India and went from there to Greece and Italy. The Romans spread the plant around their empire, and the rest of the world followed along. The British were especially taken with cucumbers and built protection in the form of little sheds and greenhouses so they could grow them in the cold climate. The English cucumber, long and slender and seedless, is a gourmet treat to this day. The Spaniards brought cucumbers to the New World, where they found good conditions for growing.

Unlike most of the Native American tribes, who lived nomadic lives, the Mandan, in what is now the Dakotas, early on established permanent villages and began a system of agriculture. The women of the tribe were the best farmers on the Great Plains. When the Europeans arrived in their villages in the early 1700s, they found that the people were growing a dozen or more varieties of corn, a great number of pumpkins, squashes, and gourds, and favorite European vegetables, including at least six kinds of beans. They were eager to trade with trappers, hunters, and explorers from Europe for new varieties for their gardens, including cucumbers and watermelons.

European settlers had brought their seeds with them to colonial America. Among them were cucumbers, sometimes called "cowcumbers," which had a mixed reputation. Some people thought they were good only for feeding the cows—hence the name. Samuel Pepys, famous English diarist, wrote on September 22, 1663, that "Mr. Newhouse is dead of eating cowcumbers, of which the other day I heard of another, I think."

Of course, the weather in New England was not much better than it was in England, and cucumbers do like warm weather and are susceptible to cold. Wait to plant your cucumbers until the soil has warmed at least to 60 degrees F. Even the lightest frost will kill young plants. Plant seeds in beds that have been enriched with compost or well-rotted manure. The reason most seed packets and instructions say to plant cucumbers, melons, and squash seeds in hills is that by mounding up the soil you guarantee that the seeds will have rapid drainage while they are getting established. These seeds will rot readily if they sit around in damp soil very long. They need full sun and no competition from tree or shrub roots. Like most vegetables, cucumbers are heavy feeders. Plant the seeds in hills and put a support in place. You can grow vining types in cages or tepees, on trellises or fences, or on a matrix of heavy twine. Bush varieties need no support. Feed your young plants every two weeks with a seaweed and fish mixture

sprayed on the leaves as well as the ground. The seaweed will help protect against disease as well as supply micronutrients. Keep a watch out for squash bugs and squash beetles. Knock those nasty little critters off into a jar of soapy water if you spy any on your morning inspection of the garden. It is often helpful to have a jar of soapy water on hand when you are looking over your veggies. Most bugs will expire in that mixture, and it is easy enough to tip them in with your fingers or a small stick if you are squeamish.

Start harvesting the cucumbers when they are the right length for their variety. Don't let them get too big, or they will lose their good taste. Keep picking to encourage new fruit set. And keep encouraging the bees and other pollinators in your garden. A jar of honey water strategically placed will bring them in and feed them as well. Without bees our gardens would be pitiful things.

One of my favorite varieties of cucumber isn't a cucumber at all. The Armenian cucumber is really a melon (*Cucumis melo*) that tastes like a cucumber, looks like a cucumber, and can be used just like a cucumber. Also known as yard-long cucumber, the Armenian cucumber has many of the characteristics of the long English cucumber. It is slender and thin-skinned and has a nice mild flavor. There is no bitterness, and the seeds are small and few. The crisp, juicy texture is characteristic of cucumber's freshness. An added benefit is that the outside is ribbed with alternating light and dark green coloration, so when you slice one, it looks as if you have done some fancy decorating.

Armenian cucumbers grow on a long vine, and while they can be grown on the ground, the fruit will be straighter and cleaner if the vine grows vertically. Any fruit lying on the ground is more susceptible to insects and other critters as well as rot and disease. These cucumbers can grow to as much as 30 inches long, but they are at their best when they are about 12 inches long. Because of their size, they make great sliced pickles. It doesn't take many to make a recipe. Bread-and-butter pickles are especially good and not as hard to make as you might think. All you really need is a big pot. I use the recipe below to make pickles from both cucumbers and squash. It is an old recipe that came from a Methodist church cookbook published in 1927.

School Boy's Delight Bread and Butter Pickles

12 medium-sized cucumbers (The fewer seeds the better. I use 6
  Armenian.)
4 medium-sized onions
4 medium green sweet peppers
7 cups sugar
6 cups cider vinegar
2 cups water
2 Tbsp. celery seed
4 Tbsp. mustard seed
1½ tsp. turmeric

Wash and thinly slice cucumbers (or squash), onions, and
  peppers.
Soak in brine water (¾ cup salt to 6 quarts water) three hours,
  drain.
Combine sugar, vinegar, water, and spices in large preserving
  kettle; boil two or three minutes; add squash mix and boil until
  clear (about 20 minutes).
Pour into hot sterilized jars and seal at once.

Another terrific heirloom cucumber is the lemon cucumber.
Introduced into the trade in 1894 in the United States by a seedsman
in Pennsylvania, this cucumber looks very much like a lemon but does
not taste like one. It is lemon-shaped and -sized with white skin heavily
striped with yellow. It is pretty to look at and very tasty to eat. The flesh
is firm, mild, and crisp. It is easy to digest and can be used in many different ways—even eaten raw off the vine as if it were an apple. It is rust
and drought resistant and extremely productive.

Cucumbers are fresh and delicious, but they are surprisingly nutritious, too, given that they taste like really bright water. They are a
source of vitamin C and a good source of vitamin A, vitamin K,
folate, potassium, manganese, magnesium, and dietary fiber. They
also contain compounds called plant sterols that have been shown to
lower cholesterol in animals. The heaviest concentration of sterols is
in the skin, so don't peel them unless necessary. In addition to all that,

cucumbers are a great aid to digestion and have a cleansing effect on the bowel. The final bonus is that they have almost no calories, so you can eat them with abandon.

Most Americans think of cucumbers as vegetables or fruits to be eaten raw, but in many parts of the world they are stewed, fried, baked, and prepared in many other ways. When you have an abundance of cucumbers and aren't in the mood to make pickles, that is the perfect time to experiment with other uses. Here is a simple and tasty side dish you can whip up in minutes.

Sautéed Cucumbers

1 Tbsp. butter
2 cucumbers, peeled, halved lengthwise, and cut into half moons
Pinch of nutmeg
Handful of herbs (Use what you have—tarragon, chives, chervil, thyme, or parsley.)
Salt and pepper

Melt the butter in a pan over medium heat. Add the cucumbers Cook for about 5 minutes, or until they have somewhat crisped up.
Add the nutmeg, herbs, salt, and pepper to the pan and mix together.
Remove from the heat and serve.

Of course, the really great thing about cucumbers is that when you have many of them, you want something cool and easy to fix. Nobody wants to stand around in the summer heating up the kitchen. The two easiest and quickest ways to serve cucumbers are also, in my opinion, the best. Both options involve slicing the cucumbers crosswise, peeling if the peel is tough, and combining with sliced onions. The first and probably most common option is to pour vinegar over the vegetables, salt and pepper, and chill. The second is to pour yogurt (or sour cream or a mix of the two) over the vegetables, salt and pepper, and chill. This second option is even better if you chop up some fresh dill or fresh mint and add it to the mix. These are quick and delicious side dishes for any meal.

A variation on sliced cucumbers in yogurt is cold cucumber soup. Wonderfully refreshing and delicious for lunch or dinner, this will make your family or your friends think you are a gourmet cook—and you don't even have to turn on the stove.

Cold Cucumber Soup

2 large cucumbers, peeled, seeded, and grated with a box grater or
  food processor
1 finely minced garlic clove
½ palmful of minced, fresh dill
1½ cups plain yogurt (Greek style is good because it is thicker, or
  you can use half yogurt and half sour cream.)
½ box organic free-range chicken broth
Salt and white pepper (if you have it, black if you don't) to taste

Combine all ingredients, stir to blend, and chill. Serve topped with
  any of the following (or combination thereof): chopped cucumber, fresh dill or mint, a dollop of sour cream or yogurt, diced
  avocado, snipped chives or green onions. Serves four.

Beans

People have an interesting relationship with beans. We talk about them as if they were the most insignificant things in the world: "He doesn't know beans about that!" "She is such a bean counter." And yet almost every early society and many late ones depended on beans as a staple in their diet: beans and rice, beans and tortillas, beans and couscous. In fact, people learned early on that combining beans and grain (wheat, corn, or rice) creates complete proteins that can keep people healthy, strong, and satisfied.

Beans have been cultivated for thousands of years throughout the world. Common garden beans began being cultivated in Peru sometime around 7000 BC; lentils and fava beans were being grown in the Middle East and Egypt shortly after that. It is interesting that so many of our common garden vegetables originated in Peru. The Incas were adventurous farmers, developing peppers, potatoes, corn, and chocolate for their tables. Beans are just one crop that was spread by Spanish explorers around the globe.

Beans have traveled so far because they are extremely adaptable and useful. There are more than four thousand varieties of beans, and each is adapted to the place where it grows. In addition to their ability to grow almost anywhere, beans can be dried and stored for years; can be eaten raw, sprouted, or cooked; and can be ground into flour, curdled into tofu, and fermented into miso. They can be a main course, side dish, soup, salad, stew, even dessert. Studies show that beans are packed with nutritious components. When combined with nuts, seeds, or grains, they form a complex, high-fiber vegetable protein. Alone, they are low in fat and high in fiber, help lower cholesterol, are high in carbohydrates, which provide energy, and are packed with essential B vitamins, manganese, and iron.

Early Native American farmers grew beans, corn, and squash—the three sacred sisters—together. They used the corn as poles on which the beans could climb while the squash wandered underneath as a ground cover. The corn provided some sun protection for the squash and beans, the beans fixed nitrogen in the soil as fertilizer for the other crops, and the squash grew into a mass of hairy leaves that were uncomfortable for critters to walk on and birds to land in. This symbiotic relationship served for generations to provide these essential food crops. It was the ability to grow these basics of life that led to the change from hunter-gatherer societies to settled communities. Europeans added other grains, such as wheat, and different beans to increase the range of possibilities. Beans are still an important element of world agriculture.

We generally classify beans by how we eat them: dry, shelled, and green (snap). Although most bean varieties can be eaten in all three stages, some are definitely better than others for specific uses. For example, many beans grown to be used dry have tough pods and aren't really tasty at the green stage. In the Southwest, many people eat pinto beans both dried and green, and while the green pods are definitely edible,

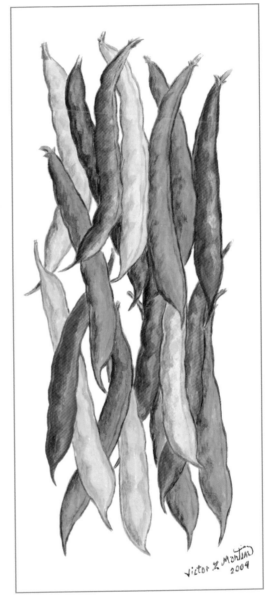

they aren't the best green beans in the world. They are a little coarse and not as tender and tasty as other beans. On the other hand, few people grow Kentucky Wonder beans for the dried seed. They are excellent green beans, however, and have been grown for generations for just that purpose.

No matter how you eat them, beans are grown the same way. They need warm soil to generate, lots of sun to grow, and a particular bacteria in the soil to really prosper. As members of the legume family they have the unique ability to grab nitrogen out of the air and fix it in the soil, thus providing fertility for themselves and other plants growing around them. This ability, however, depends on the presence of rhizobia bacteria in the ground. Once the bacteria are in the ground, they will remain for a very long time, but if your garden is new or you aren't sure, you can buy a cheap inoculant to sprinkle on your seeds to make certain that necessary bacteria are present in your soil. It is an organic substance and serves no other purpose except to help beans provide their own fertilizer. In addition, your bean crop will be much more productive and healthy if the bacterium is present, so when you decide to grow beans, buy some inoculant. Ask your local nursery to get some if they don't carry it. You might also ask if the organic fertilizer you are using has the bacteria in it. Some do.

Another thing that garden experts don't always tell you is that while you must wait until after frost is past to plant your beans, you can wait too long. Everyone wants to get the garden in early, not only because we want fresh veggies in a hurry, but also because once it gets really hot many vegetables won't produce. Beans are one example of that.

Planting beans in midsummer will result in disappointment. Green beans like warm but not hot weather in which to develop, and beans meant to be dried are the same. The traditional date in Europe, the southern United States, and many other places for planting beans is Good Friday. It is supposed to be good luck to plant on that date and is also supposed to guarantee a good crop. It wouldn't hurt to check with your local extension agent to make sure of the best date in your climate. My grandfather always planted beans on Good Friday in North Texas even though we usually had a cold snap at Easter. He also planted by the moon—and he managed to feed his family of eight from a small backyard garden. Of course, when I was little I thought that garden was huge! I can remember looking down the rows and thinking they must go on for miles. Now when I drive by the lot where it grew, I can't believe so much food came out of that little space.

Plant your beans in a sunny spot and put supports in place if you are growing pole beans. Pole beans will grow on tepees, trellises, cages, or any other upright, including corn. Bush beans can stand on their own. Don't put a high-nitrogen fertilizer on beans, as that will encourage leaf growth instead of beans. Use a good organic fertilizer that has phosphorus and potassium as well as trace minerals. A mulch of compost around the plants when they are established and regular watering with compost tea will encourage heavy production. Don't let your plants dry out if there is no rain. Water well, at least once a week.

Pick your beans for green use when they are young and tender. When they are producing you'll probably need to pick every day. Pick snap beans before you notice seeds swelling. Harvest shell beans when the pods are plump but before they start turning brown. Leave dry beans on the plant until the seeds are hard and the pods are dry. Once the plant quits producing, add it to the compost heap.

Most of the heirloom beans you find are used at the dry stage because they are the longest keepers and better providers for feeding the family year-round. Of the varieties used green, most of them are pole beans. Kentucky Wonder, Empress, Bountiful, and other varieties are delicious snap beans that have been around a long time. Almost every region, and in some regions almost every family, has a bean that has grown there for a long time. Old farmers save their seeds and the beans become better adapted through time. If you can find a bean that has grown in your neighborhood for a while, try that one.

The hotter the climate, the better dry beans will do and the shorter the season for green beans. As a result, fresh green beans seem like a real luxury to me since our Texas summer gets too hot too quickly. I prefer to grow slender-pod beans that grow on bushes, because the pole beans take extra time growing vines when they could be producing beans. In hot climates you have to get the most out of those few pleasant days of spring before summer gets serious. I also like to mix green, purple, and wax (yellow) beans so that there is some variety in the kitchen. The French seem particularly adept at developing nice, long, firm green beans. Roc D'Or yellow wax beans and others in the *haricot vert* group are slender, brittle, and yummy. I try different varieties every year to see which ones do best.

While green beans are a tasty springtime treat, dried beans are a staple of many people's diets. Full of nutrients and protein, dried beans have been feeding people year-round for millennia. Beans eaten fresh in the shell stage are delicious and to be enjoyed fresh, but dried beans will keep you going when the garden plays out.

One indication of the many different kinds of beans around is all those recipes for fifteen-bean soup. Dried beans either as soup or just as beans are great winter comfort food. Be sure to cook your dried beans thoroughly. Some red-colored dried beans have a toxic covering that will make you feel bad if they are eaten raw or undercooked. Beans should be soaked or precooked before cooking for a fairly long time until they are very tender. If you forget to start your dried beans soaking the night before you want to cook them, you can accomplish the same goal by precooking them. Put the beans in a pan of cold water and bring them to a boil. Boil hard for 1–2 minutes, then cover the pan and turn off the heat. Let them sit for one hour, then pour off the water and start over. This time cook as you would if you had soaked the beans—until they are tender and delicious.

Then there was that legend going around a while back about how you couldn't salt beans until they were almost done or they would stay hard or never get done or some such. That has proven false, and some say adding salt in the beginning helps the beans cook faster. Still, there is no reason to salt them early. You want to add salt when you can taste them and see if the seasoning is right. Other flavors people like added to dried beans are pepper, onion, cumin, sage, bay, and more. Fresh snap beans go well with sage, dill, and thyme.

One of the easiest and most delicious recipes in the world is a bean salad made from whatever beans you have on hand—green beans, wax beans, cooked dried beans—plus oil, vinegar, a pinch of sugar, salt, pepper, onion, and peppers. Toss and refrigerate. Taste for flavor and enjoy. You can change it up to create a Mexican flavor by adding chili peppers, lime juice, cilantro, and cumin. For a Mediterranean flair, add feta cheese, marinated artichoke hearts, and black olives. Create your own by adding pasta, rice, avocado, or whatever you like best. It is hard to mess up beans.

Peas

In the vegetable kingdom some families sort of blur into each other. Common garden beans are *Phaseolus vulgaris;* lima beans are *Phaseolus lunatus;* fava beans are *Vicia faba;* runner beans are *Phaseolus coccineus;* long beans are *Vigna unguiculata;* garbanzos are *Cicer arietinum;* lentils are *Lens culinaris;* and soybeans are *Glycine max.* They are all called "beans" and are members of the legume family, as are peas. Peas come in different types and species as well. The green garden pea is *Pisum sativum,* and the field pea, with its many colors and types, is the same species as long beans—*Vigna unguiculata*—although it used to be classified as a *Phaseolus.* Scientific naming can be confusing, and they keep changing the rules. But as gardeners and eaters we don't really need a Latin name to legitimize a plant.

Peas come in two styles: green (garden), which grow best in cool climates, and field, which grow best in hot climates. Being human, we develop all sorts of peculiar prejudices based on what we ate when we were kids. My Yankee husband insists that field peas are fit only for feeding livestock. A native Texan, I'm inclined to think there is much ado about not much when it comes to fresh green peas.

Field peas come in a variety of colors and sizes. Probably the best known is the black-eyed pea, but there are also red-eyes, pink-eyes, crowder peas, cream peas, and others are that are eaten shelled or dried. Field peas came to the United States with slaves brought from Africa—thus their importance as an element of "soul food." Eating black-eyed peas on New Year's Day is thought to bring good luck in the coming year in the South, although the tradition dates much further back to ancient Babylon.

Peas are often grown as a cover crop and as a way to increase fertility and hold down weed growth in fallow fields. Because they can fix nitrogen in the soil, they are good for improving any soil. Of course, they require the necessary bacteria to do that, so, as described above for beans, the bacteria should be added when peas are first planted.

Gardeners usually pick the first bunch of field peas and eat them shelled, cooked with salt, pepper, oil or ham, and lemon juice. Lots of people sprinkle the cooked peas with pepper sauce (vinegar with hot chili peppers in the bottle). A popular dish in the Caribbean Islands is hoppin' John, which can be made with either shelled or dried cooked peas combined with rice and pork. A favorite for New Year's Day parties is Texas caviar, which is cooked peas marinated in a vinaigrette of oil, vinegar (or lemon juice), onions, garlic, peppers, salt, and black pepper and served cold.

Black-eyed peas are versatile and nutritious. They are an excellent source of several minerals, vitamin A, folate, and other nutrients. Fresh peas can be frozen and dried peas stored at room temperature. They are easy to grow and easy to eat. What are those Yankees thinking?

They are thinking, of course, of green garden peas, sometimes called English peas, which are small spheres contained in fat little pods. Peas grow and produce best when the temperature ranges between 55 and 65 degrees F. Summer heat does them in quickly. They grow in rich, well-drained soil in full sun. The vining types send out tendrils that coil around any available support and can grow to a few feet high. A traditional support for peas is pruned tree branches pushed into the soil. Metal fences and twine or netting supported by a frame can be used for the same purpose. Again, rhizobia bacteria are necessary for peas to produce well.

Fresh green peas are commonly eaten boiled or steamed with mint added for flavor. Salt and pepper and butter are added at the last minute. Some varieties are grown for their edible pods; snow peas and sugar

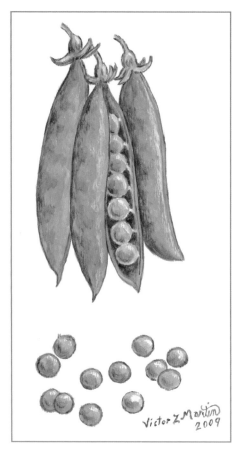

or snap peas are eaten whole before the pod reaches maturity. Thomas Jefferson grew more than thirty cultivars of peas on his estate, and these peas are widely used in all parts of the world. In India, fresh peas are used in many dishes and eaten raw, as they are sweet when fresh off the bush.

Dried peas are most often made into soup—the traditional split pea soup. In England, dried peas are cooked and mashed and known as "mushy peas." This delightful sounding dish is particularly popular at fish and chips shops and as a side dish with meat pies. It was the English, after all, who came up with the children's song "Pease porridge hot, pease porridge cold, / Pease porridge in the pot, nine days old." Sounds yummy, right? After a while we shortened the name from pease to pea.

Leaves and sprouts of pea plants are also edible. The Japanese use garden pea sprouts in stir-fries, and they occasionally appear on salad buffet tables. The sprouts are sweet and delicious. You can make your own by soaking pea seeds in fresh water for 8–12 hours. Rinse and set aside on a damp paper towel or clean muslin or cotton cloth or in a sprouter, if you own one. Rinse again in another 12 hours. Repeat the process until you have sprouted peas. You can use the same process to sprout black-eyed peas. Pea sprouts have much more flavor and substance than the more common alfalfa sprouts, which are mostly stem.

Potatoes

As the Irish and my younger daughter Jenny discovered, it is possible
to sustain yourself and even thrive on a diet made up almost entirely
of potatoes. When Jenny was a teenager, she decided that she needed
to lose weight, and she did so by restricting her diet to potatoes—
mashed, baked, steamed, canned, and frozen. It may not sound like the
best weight-loss plan, but it worked for her, and she's still very fond
of potatoes and is nice and trim besides. (She does, however, eat other
foods now.) The eighteenth- and nineteenth-century Irish, on the other
hand, ate potatoes because that's what they could grow in their rocky,
cold, poor soil. They made the mistake, however, of not including a little
diversity in their planting. When the blight began to spread in the 1840s,
it spread to all the fields growing the same kind of potatoes.

Like many of our favorite vegetables, Irish or white potatoes (*Solanum
tuberosum*) originated in the Andes Mountains of South America. It
is amazing that so many plants came from that place where the soil is
poor and the temperatures fluctuate between extremes. The tough pre-
Columbian farmers discovered and cultivated the potato some seven
thousand years ago. When the conquistadores tramped through Peru in
the 1500s, they started the transport of potatoes to the far corners of the
world.

The Spanish took the potato home and gave it to the poor folks. It wasn't considered classy enough for the, well, classy folks. Oddly, lobsters had the same reputation for years. They were given to prisoners and pensioners and other people who were willing to eat almost anything. One of the reasons potatoes were given to the poor was because the rich were afraid that they might be poisonous: "Let poor old Juan eat it and see if he dies!" Potatoes are members of the nightshade family, a group of plants that do contain poisonous elements. The leaves are poisonous, and a potato left too long in the light will begin to turn green. The green skin contains a substance called solanine, which can cause the potato to taste bitter and cause illness in humans.

It was the Irish who recognized that this rugged crop would produce abundant, nutritious food, something hard to come by in Ireland. Unlike any other major crop, potatoes contain most of the vitamins needed for sustenance, and they are efficient as well. Potatoes can sustain ten people on only one acre of land. In the early 1800s there was a boom in population in Ireland because of this source of nutrition.

In France, the potato was still suspect until an intellectual, Antoine Augustine Parmentier, saw the nutritional benefits and productive capacity of the crop. He acquired a plot of miserable land on the outskirts of Paris and proceeded to plant fifty acres in potatoes. During the day he set a guard over the plot. Obviously, curious folks decided this crop must be something extremely valuable to merit such protection. The guard was relaxed at night, and soon the potato began appearing in farms and on tables across France. In time the potato returned to its native American soil and became a staple in our diet. We forget that it has only been with us for a few hundred years.

Although potatoes are relatively cheap at the grocery store, like every other vegetable, homegrown ones are light-years better. Growing potatoes is easy, and because they can grow in cool seasons, they are grown in warm climates before the main gardening season begins. Potatoes are planted from chunks of potatoes or small potatoes that have been allowed to ripen and develop "eyes." These seed potatoes can be bought from local feed stores, nurseries, or farmers who save their own seed. If you can find an organic source, shop there.

Before planting, put your seed potatoes in a bright spot and maybe some of the eyes will begin to sprout. Dig your garden spot well and remove any rocks. Plant your potatoes in a trench or holes about 6 inches deep and cover them with good soil. Keep them watered if there is not sufficient rain, but don't let the soil become soggy. Potatoes will rot if the soil is too wet. Once the potatoes begin to sprout and poke through the ground, hill up the soil around the stems. Keep doing this for a few weeks while the plants grow. This practice will result in better and larger potatoes, because the potatoes grow along the stems underground, and the more stem underground, the more potatoes. Don't bury the leaves, just the stems.

As the potatoes begin to mature, you can stick your hand into the soil and rob a few of those new potatoes that are so creamy and tasty that you won't believe your taste buds. Let the plants continue to grow until they flower or until they begin to look worn out and wilted. All the books I've read say harvest after the plants bloom, but my plants almost never bloom. So I simply wait until they look as if they are done and start digging. Be careful when you dig so that you don't cut the potatoes.

There are other ways to grow potatoes that don't even require soil. I've seen descriptions of methods in which potatoes are grown in old tires filled with straw or piled-up cages filled with leaves. The tires are not a great idea because they contain chemicals you don't want in your food, but perhaps you could find a similar but cleaner alternative. I've never tried any of these methods, so I can't recommend them, but they sound interesting. I think they are employed in cooler climates than mine in order to warm up more quickly. Warming up is not a problem in Central Texas.

Picking the variety of potato that will work best for you is usually accomplished best by asking around. In my neighborhood everybody grows red or white, and you can find them at most feed stores in January. Wonderful varieties are available in yellow and blue and in exotic sizes and shapes. Our heavy clay soil is not the best for potatoes, so I stick to the old standards. A few years ago I tried some fingerlings from Maine. They were not a success.

The rules of local and tried-and-true work best when choosing seed potatoes. On the other hand, if you have access to some nifty new types of potatoes grown organically by local farmers and offered at farm stands or markets, give them a try. The delicacy of taste in homegrown potatoes will astound you.

Like Jenny, I enjoy potatoes almost any way, and tender new potatoes need only gentle cooking and a bit of butter to create a springtime feast. When the weather gets hotter and potatoes older, however, I always return to my Aunt LaVeda's vichyssoise. It is a cold and delicious treat any time of the year except in the winter, when it becomes comforting warm potato soup.

LaVeda's Potato Soup/Vichyssoise

2 cups sliced potatoes (Select a firm, moist variety like Red LaSoda.)

6–8 green onions, chopped (include tops)

3 Tbsp. butter

4 cups chicken broth

2–4 stalks celery, *not* chopped

4 sprigs parsley

⅛ tsp. white pepper

1 cup half-and-half

1 tsp. Worcestershire sauce

Salt to taste

Melt butter in a large sauce pan over medium heat and add chopped onions. Cook for about five minutes, stirring often to make sure they don't burn.

Add broth, potatoes, celery, parsley, and pepper. Cook over low heat for about 30 minutes or until potatoes are tender.

Discard celery and parsley.

Puree the vegetables or mash thoroughly if you like a few lump

Stir cream and Worcestershire sauce into mixture. Taste and adjust seasonings. This soup is great hot or cold. Garnish with chopped chives.

Although many people use the names sweet potato and yam interchangeably, they are completely different plants. Yams (*Dioscorea* sp.) are plants native to the South Pacific which require near-tropical conditions in which to thrive. Sweet potatoes (*Ipomoea batatas*), on the other hand, will produce well in most areas of the United States.

It is a shame that so many of us eat sweet potatoes only at Thanksgiving and Christmas. They are highly nutritious vegetables, rich in vitamins A and C, and easy to grow and store. One of the reasons many home gardeners do not attempt sweet potatoes is that they are not readily available at garden centers. Sweet potatoes are grown from slips—rooted cuttings with leaves in place—rather than from seed or dried tubers. Cuttings are available from a few nurseries and feed stores and also can be ordered from some mail order catalogs, but you can also start your own slips from potatoes you purchase at a farmer's market or store. (Sources are listed in the back of this book.)

Select potatoes that are grown in your area, if possible, and buy from an organic grower. These potatoes will most likely be well adapted to your garden and will do well. There are several methods of preparing slips.

1. Select firm potatoes and cut in half lengthwise. Lay the cut side down in a pan containing a shallow layer of wet sand. Cover the pan with plastic wrap and store it in a warm spot until sprouts appear on the potatoes. Remove the plastic wrap and let the sprouts continue to grow until they have 4–5 leaves and are 4–8 inches tall with roots. At this point you can remove the sprouts from the remaining potato and plant.

2. Place a whole potato in a jar with water covering the bottom inch of the potato. (Many of us did this in kindergarten.) When leaves appear above the roots, remove the slip with its roots and plant either outdoors or in a deep flat or pot to keep it growing until time to transplant.

3. If you know someone who grows sweet potatoes, or you want to grow your own slips for next year from this year's crop, you can take cuttings from vine tips in the fall just before the first frost. Cut off 3- to 4-inch sections from the end of a healthy vine and place the cuttings in water. Keep them in a warm place, and when roots appear, transplant to a 6-inch pot. These pots can sit

in a warm, sunny window throughout the winter and serve as houseplants until it is time to plant outdoors in the spring. You will probably be able to make further cuttings from these plants as spring approaches.

Sweet potatoes are warm-weather plants that are very sensitive to frost, so they should not be planted until the soil is thoroughly warm in the spring. Generally, a month after the last frost date is a good time to plant your slips. The plants grow best between 75 degrees and 85 degrees F.

Sweet potatoes need to grow either in a raised bed or in deep mounded ridges. They prefer sandy soil but will do well in other types of soil if it is well prepared. When you prepare the bed in the spring, dig deeply and remove any rocks or other impediments to growth. The potatoes do not like competition for space. Place 1–2 inches of compost in your ridge, and then mound at least 10 inches of soil on top of the compost. One method of planting is to cover your ridge with black plastic and make slits in the plastic in which to place your slips. The plastic warms the soil quickly and keeps it warm while at the same time keeping the soil in place and the weeds down while your young vines establish themselves.

Place your rooted cuttings four to five inches into the soil and 12–18 inches apart. A thin layer of rock phosphate at root level will provide needed phosphorus as the young plants grow. If you are using the black plastic method, cut slits for your plants and poke them into the earth with a rounded stick, such as a broom handle. Water thoroughly after they are planted. Once established, sweet potatoes are very drought hardy. Keep weeds away from the plants until the vines are large enough to shade out weeds themselves.

Pests are generally not a big problem with sweet potatoes. An occasional lone vandal, such as a flea beetle or weevil, will gnaw on the leaves, but they do little damage to the plant as a whole. The sweet potatoes will grow as the vine grows, and the vine will grow until frost. Don't wait for the vines to wilt before harvesting as you would regular potatoes. Most experts agree that frost on the vines harms the potatoes, so you should dig them before the first frost. If you have nice, loose soil, you can steal potatoes as they mature and leave the vine intact.

To harvest, remove the plastic, if you used it, and dig with a pitch-fork. Select a dry day for harvesting when both air and soil are low in moisture. Begin digging several inches away from the plant so you don't pierce the potatoes. Let the potatoes lay on the ground to cure for several hours, then brush off clinging dirt with your hands. Do not wash them until you're ready to cook them.

That is the official story. The true story is that sweet potatoes are very happy to grow and will do more than their part. A few years ago I bought a big box full of sweet potatoes from a farmer who'd brought them to the market from East Texas, where they grow happily. We ate them and ate them and then they were gone. Or so I thought. About mid-July I moved a garden hat on the back porch, and guess what I found. A small pile of sweet potatoes had been forgotten. They had all sprouted and were piti-ful, shriveled-looking things with straggly stems and leaves.

Oh well, I thought, compost or garden? Since it was mid-July and most of my spring crops had played out, I stuck them in the ground and ignored them aside from a little water now and then. I didn't prepare the soil, didn't fertilize, and didn't hover. By October sweet potato vines cov-ered the raised bed where they were planted and drifted off into the grass on every side. When we dug them to see if in fact there were potatoes there, we were amazed. It was a great bunch of potatoes, and that year I didn't have to seek out the farmer with the East Texas potatoes.

My husband Bob is an imaginative person, and every September he thinks it is time to start a new business. Many of these ideas never see the light of day, but he has fun planning. A recent great idea was the Yam Van. The Yam Van would be a vehicle (van or bus or truck) with a giant sweet potato on top. It would travel around to street fairs and sell baked sweet potatoes with a wide array of toppings. There would, of course, be the standard butter, but that is just the beginning: maple syrup, marsh-mallows, coconut, pecans, chili powder, chocolate bits, pineapple chunks, cinnamon imperials, and whatever else sounds good. At summer fairs it would be a delicious, nutritious, and hand-held treat. At winter fairs it would be all that plus a hand-warmer. He's looking for a theme song.

In the meantime, your homegrown sweet potatoes will offer many delightful meals. They are wonderful simply baked and slathered with butter, fried, boiled, or (of course) candied for the holidays.

Tomatillos

I'm surprised at how many people still don't know what tomatillos are. Back in about 1990 I found a few tomatillo plants at a nursery and decided that would be my peculiar plant of the season. I loved green salsa, and whenever I had seen tomatillos at the grocery store, they were very expensive. So I figured they must be hard to grow. In fact, they were incredibly easy to grow. I had tomatillos coming out my ears.

There is only so much salsa a person can eat, so I started looking for other things to do with my bountiful crop—and found almost nothing. The short version is that I became fascinated and wrote my first gardening book: *Tomatillos: A Gardener's Dream, a Cook's Delight.* A combination growing and cooking guide, the book was originally designed as an interesting project and something I could give relatives for Christmas. It soon caught on, however, and we've been selling it ever since. As a result of that book I was featured on *The New Garden* television show, which led to my being a host on that series, led to my editing *The New Garden Journal,* and led to my starting *Homegrown Magazine,* which led to other gardening books. So, in fact, this whole part of my life is thanks to a small, rather obscure fruit from Mexico.

What I thought was a

local crop turns out to be of interest to people all over the world. We've sent books (the originals contained seeds) to Norway, Denmark, Japan, and a lot of other unlikely places. Apparently tomatillos have a much larger range than I thought, and lots of people love their tangy taste.

Tomatillos (*Physalis philadelphica*) are not tomatoes, although they are relatives. They are also not hot. Those are the two major misconceptions about this little fruit. Tomatillos are sometimes called "husk tomatoes," which keeps the confusion going. They grow inside a papery husk and have an almost lemony flavor. Their flavor is, really, all their own.

Tomatillos probably originated in Central or South America, but it was the Aztecs in Mexico who began cultivation of tomatillos and made them part of their cuisine. The Tarahumara Indians of Mexico use wild tomatillos in their cooking, as they have from time immemorial. The Zunis of northern New Mexico have cultivated them for centuries. The conquistadores took tomatillos home to Spain along with tomatoes, but they never really caught on in Europe as the tomato did. In fact, tomatillos only became popular in mainstream American cooking during the past twenty years or so.

Tomatillos grow on a sprawling plant that resists containment. Unlike tomatoes, which grow well in cages, tomatillos prefer to stay close to the ground and wander. The small yellow blossoms grow into little paper lantern–shaped husks in which the fruit grows. Tomatillos come in both green and purple, and as they grow, they burst through the papery husk to reveal plump little cherry-sized fruit. They are ready to pick when they break through the husk. Many grocery store tomatillos are yellow and dried out. They have been around too long. Pick both green and purple varieties when they pop the husk and are firm and smooth.

Growing tomatillos is easy, but not as easy as I first thought. Apparently there are good years and not so good years for tomatillos. And nobody knows why. Some summers there are more tomatillos than you can harvest. Others, the plants set hardly a fruit. So you have to experiment. Plant in full sun in rich soil. Spray regularly with liquid seaweed and other organic fertilizers to encourage bloom and fruit set.

Unlike tomatoes, tomatillos will set fruit when it is very hot, so you can plant the seeds directly in the garden when frosts are over. They will sprout in about a week and grow quickly into good-sized plants. Water and fertilize as you do tomatoes and pick the fruit regularly when they start ripening. In a good year you'll have tomatillos all summer long. They really like hot weather so don't expect early crops. Wait until it is hot and then start harvesting your crop. It should go on until the first frost of the fall.

You may be surprised to learn that tomatillos are very nutritious. One medium raw tomatillo contains only 11 calories but has 91 milligrams of potassium, 2.4 milligrams of calcium, 4 milligrams of vitamin C, 2.38 milligrams of folic acid, and 39 international units of vitamin A. And nobody eats just one!

Store fresh tomatillos in their husk in the refrigerator. When you are ready to use them, remove the husk and wash away the sticky substances on the surface of the fruit. Then you can chop them and use them any way you want. The most common use is in salsa. If you make salsa with tomatoes, you can use the same recipe except that you will substitute tomatillos instead of tomatoes. The results will be very different. The tomato salsa will be sweet and hot. The tomatillo salsa will be tangy and hot. If you like, you can make a salsa with both tomatillos and tomatoes. You can also make salsa either raw or cooked. Raw will be tangier, since cooking brings out the sweetness in the fruit. Here is my favorite recipe.

Salsa Verde

1 pound tomatillos
1 cup chopped onion
4 cloves garlic
1½ tsp. salt
½ cup oil
1 cup water
½ cup cilantro (or to taste)
2 serrano peppers (or to taste)

Cut tomatillos in half and place in blender or food processor with other ingredients, reserving 2 tablespoons of oil. Heat reserved oil over medium heat in heavy pan, and then add purée. Simmer on low heat for 10–12 minutes. Serve as a dip with tortilla chips, use in a recipe, or freeze for later use.

I usually freeze a bunch of salsa when there are plenty of fruit available. It can be used later in lots of recipes—meat dishes, desserts, salads, and preserves. Tomatillos are fun to experiment with in the kitchen in those years when you have a bountiful crop. The next time you bake an apple pie, add a handful of chopped tomatillos to the apples. You'll be pleasantly surprised.

These days' tomatillos are not nearly so expensive at the grocery store and you can sometimes find them at farmer's markets as well. If you don't want to grow them, buy some and give them a try. Because they are old plants that haven't been popular enough to be messed with, almost every tomatillo you find will be an heirloom. That means that they are generally very good at reseeding themselves. After that first year I planted them, I had babies coming up for several years from the previous year's crop, and all I had to do was transplant them into the spot where I wanted them to grow. One year I had plants coming up around the compost heap. You've got to love a plant that wants to grow that much!

If you don't trust that your tomatillos will reseed, or if you want enough to share with friends, it is easy to save the seeds. Pick the fruit when it is completely ripe and ready to fall off the vine. Thoroughly mash the fruit and mix it with an equal amount of water. Keep the mixture at room temperature for several days, and stir the mess every day. Good seed will settle to the bottom of your dish. The rest of the stuff will ferment. Pour off the water, pulp, and seeds that rise to the top and discard. Wash the seeds that settle and let them dry on coffee filters. Once dry, they can be stored in paper or plastic envelopes.

Pests have little interest in tomatillos. Maybe it's because the fruit is green and doesn't call attention to itself as those gaudy red tomatoes do. Maybe it's because the bugs really like hybrids better than native heirlooms. Or maybe it's a gift for gardeners to make up for all the plagues that beset us every spring and summer. In any case, the worst problem I've had with tomatillos is that some bugs chew around on a few leaves now and then.

Garlic and Onions

I mentioned earlier that when we first moved to the country we found clumps of garlic growing in the ditches up and down the back roads. The highway department kept the major highways too tidy for volunteers to thrive, but the side roads where old farmhouses once stood and where the rain had washed garlic from the gardens into the ditches were a great source of new plants.

After some research I learned that this ditch garlic is actually rocambole garlic, also known as serpent garlic. As the plant matures, this type sends up a stalk that coils around and makes big loops before putting out a round flower head on top. This particular garlic has very large bulbs—almost as big as those of elephant garlic (which isn't really garlic at all, but a kind of leek). The cloves are also large and have a mild flavor. Garlic flavor ranges from very hot to mild, and I like the mild, which is very garlicky without being very hot.

Garlic makes bulbs to which are attached small bulblets. Some of these bulblets almost always get pulled away from the main bulb and left in the soil at harvest, thus planting the next year's crop. Of course, to ensure a good crop next year, you should plant some cloves every fall. October is a good month for planting garlic, but like many old plants, garlic is very forgiving. You can plant it almost any month of the year when the soil is workable. My two-year-old granddaughter and I planted one bed with garlic one spring after the days had begun to get warm but it was too early to plant tender crops. Wanting to get her interested in gardening as soon as possible, I suggested planting garlic, which she thought was great fun. Although it was officially too late to plant for that season, we still had a very respectable crop. Simply poke a clove, pointy end up, into the soil and walk away.

Garlic will grow in almost any soil and requires very little care. I've never had a pest problem with garlic, and in fact, it serves as pest control for other plants nearby. Many fruit growers plant garlic around the base of their trees to keep pests away. You can also make a spray of pulverized garlic to deter pests in the garden.

When the flowers at the top of the stalk open and mature, the bulbs are ready to be pulled or dug, depending on how loose your soil is. Let the bulbs lie outside in a shady place while they cure. The outside will become dry and papery. Then the bulbs can be stored in a spot with good air circulation. A basket is a good container.

Garlic has a long and distinguished history as a culinary, medicinal, and magical plant. It has been grown throughout the world for so long that no one knows where it originated. An Egyptian medical papyrus from the sixteenth century lists twenty-two remedies employing garlic for everything from heart disease and worms to tumors, headaches, and bites. In fact, ancient Egyptians seem to have worshiped garlic. Clay models of garlic bulbs were found in the tomb of Tutankhamen. Ancient Olympic athletes chewed garlic to build strength, and for centuries the Chinese have made a garlic tea designed to relieve a wide range of ailments. Of course we all know that vampires hate garlic. In folklore there is some confusion whether garlic is related to demons or keeps demons away. One myth says that as Satan left the Garden of Eden, garlic sprang up in his left footsteps and onions in the right. Maybe that confusion stems from the belief that garlic is a great aphrodisiac. For centuries garlic has been known as a potent disease preventative. It has been found to thin the blood, have strong antibacterial properties, and serve as a tonic for good health. The downside is that eating a lot of garlic causes bad breath and garlicky smelling sweat.

American chefs and food connoisseurs frowned on garlic until the 1940s. Until that time garlic was thought of as an ethnic ingredient. Perhaps because of the return of soldiers from World War II and their expanded culinary tastes, garlic soon became a major ingredient in the American kitchen. Cooks learned that gently sautéing garlic makes it sweet and delicious, while burning it makes it bitter and unpleasant. Today Americans alone consume more than 250 million pounds of garlic a year.

Garlic festivals are held throughout the country, with competitions to see how many different ways garlic can be used. The grandfather of the garlic festival is held in Gilroy, California. There, garlic is served in everything from soup to ice cream. Here is their recipe:

Gilroy Garlic Ice Cream

2 cups whole milk
1 clove garlic, minced
1 vanilla bean, split in half and seeds scraped out and reserved
1 cup heavy cream
1½ cups granulated sugar
8 egg yolks

Put milk, garlic, vanilla pod, and seeds in a saucepan. Bring to a boil over medium heat and remove immediately.

In mixing bowl, whisk the cream, sugar, and egg yolks until combined. Whisking constantly, slowly strain the hot milk mixture into the egg and sugar mixture.

Return the mixture to the pan and stir continuously over low heat until it thickens slightly and coats the back of a spoon, about 10–12 minutes. Do not boil.

Pour into a bowl and chill over an ice bath. Pour into ice cream machine and churn until done. Freeze until ready to serve. Makes 1 quart of ice cream.

One of my favorite demonstrations of the wisdom of organic gardening includes garlic. Some people will say that putting poisons on the yard does no harm; they sink into the soil and have no effect on pets or people. To show that what's on the ground transfers to people, we ask some-one to put a piece of garlic in their sock, wear it around a little while, and see what happens. What happens is that within a short time they will taste garlic in their mouths. What gets on your feet gets into your system. Even if it isn't as tasty as garlic, it is there and is having an effect.

There are two basic types of garlic—softneck or hardneck. Just as their name indicates, softneck has a pliable center stem that can be woven into those attractive garlic braids that people use to decorate their homes. Hardneck varieties (including my ditch garlic) are best stored just as bulbs. Cut off the stems and add them to the compost heap. The flower heads on my garlic dry naturally and are very nice dried bouquets. I put them in a big stoneware vase on the front porch after I cut them from the bulbs and let them air dry. Indoors they smell a little too garlicky when they are fresh, but outdoors there is no problem. Once they are dry, the scent becomes very faint, and you can bring them inside for dried arrangements.

It is relatively easy to find heirloom varieties of garlic even if your neighborhood ditches aren't full of it. Many farmers at farmer's markets grow old types, and you can plant any of those. Online sources are also available. Experiment with types to see which ones you prefer. All are easy to grow, healthy to use, and grow their own seed. The garlic at the grocery store often comes from China and has weak flavor. It is also usu-ally treated with a growth retardant so it isn't good to use as seed. Try to buy all your garlic locally until you are able to grow your own.

Garlic (*Allium sativa*) and onions (*A. cepa*) are kissing cousins (if both kissers eat them, they don't notice the odor). It is impossible to imagine most of the cuisines of the world without this dynamic duo. How many recipes start, "Chop onions and garlic and sauté . . ."? There are some good new varieties of big onion, one of the best the Texas 1015 yellow developed by Texas A&M University, but the old bunching onions are still great additions to any garden and kitchen.

As the name implies, bunching onions grow in a cluster. You start out with what looks like one green onion and end up with a whole handful of nice, juicy green onions. Also known as Welsh onions, these perennial plants never make big, round onions, but their bulbs and stalks are fla-vorful and can be used in any recipe calling for onions. Extremely hardy

Victor Z. Martin
2003

and evergreen in most regions, bunching onions can withstand temperatures as low as zero degrees F. They will grow in full sun or partial shade and will keep going year after year. Just make sure you stick one onion back in the ground if you pull up the whole bunch. You can also harvest individual onions without pulling up the bunch.

Bunching onions can be sown from seeds or from plants. If you have a neighbor or friend who grows them, that's your best source, but you can often find them at local nurseries or feed stores. They are also available online. They can be planted in either spring or fall. Most of these onions have been in cultivation since the 1800s and are reliable garden plants that produce onions almost year-round.

Another member of the onion family is the shallot (*A. ascalonicum*). This plant, like bunching onions, forms a cluster of underground bulbs from each bulb planted, but in the case of shallots, you use the bulbs instead of the stems. Shallots have a nice mild taste that is sort of a cross between onion and garlic and is a darling of chefs. When you sauté a pan of chopped shallots, you get a sweet and savory mixture that adds subtle flavor to any dish.

One grower here in Central Texas has rescued an heirloom variety of shallot that was brought here in the nineteenth century. Kevin Lundgren received the gift of shallots from a neighbor whose parents had brought them from Germany. The neighbor encouraged him to keep the crop going, since she was old and in failing health. Her garden had been neglected for several years. Lundgren planted seven plants at his certified organic farm in the Lund community and has built that original stock to more than half a million plants (see the whole story at www.organicmediaonline.org). These shallots are wonderfully adapted to the place they have been growing for more than one hundred years and are an example of how sturdy heirloom varieties can be.

Plant individual shallot bulbs in late fall, and they will be ready for harvest in early spring. Plant the bulbs so that the tip is just at soil level and add a little mulch on top. If seed stalks appear along with leaves, remove the stalk to concentrate energy in the bulbs. Harvest and dry as you would large onions. Store in a cool, dark place.

Garlic and onions are standards in the kitchen and in the garden. Finding old, reliable varieties will make growing and using them fun and interesting and keep those varieties available for the next round of gardeners and cooks.

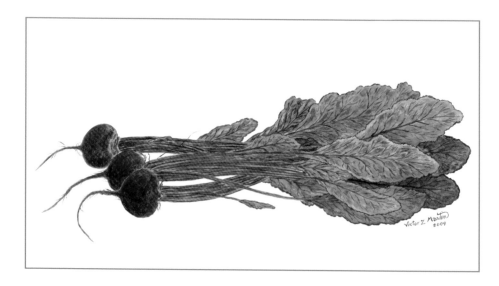

Roots

Do you think of root crops as boring, old-fashioned, and not very
trendy? Well, maybe so, but they don't deserve their shabby reputation.
Root vegetables are among the most economical, nutritious, easy-to-
grow, and long-lasting plants you can put in your garden and your
kitchen. All of them can be grown from seed, saving the price of costlier
transplants. They also are adapted to all climates; you can grow them in
the winter in the South and in the summer in the North and somewhere
in between . . . in between.

At one time Americans were simply crazy about **turnips** (*Brassica rapa*).
In an 1840 seed catalog from Rochester, New York, dozens of varieties were
offered. Today we find three or four. It's too bad turnips have gone out
of style, for the roots and tops are extremely rich in vitamins A, C, and K
and contain lots of beneficial minerals as well. When we eat tomatoes and
iceberg lettuce in the winter, we're missing out on nutrients our ancestors
got from the goodies stored in their root cellars. The standard purple-top
white globe turnip has been grown since the mid-1800s with great success.

During World War II, however, soldiers who were taken captive were
forced to live on a diet of turnips. The father of one of my friends was in
a POW camp in the Pacific, and he would not allow a turnip in the house

after that experience. A steady diet of turnips would turn anyone against them, but it is a reminder that they are full of nutrients and will keep you going even if you don't like the taste any longer.

I love turnips fresh from the garden, boiled and served with butter, salt, and pepper. The big, woody turnips available at grocery stores without greens and sometimes covered in wax will confirm any bad opinion you might have about this vegetable. But fresh turnips are mild and flavorful. If you buy them at a market, be sure they still have their fresh greens attached. You can also eat the greens, and they are good for you. I personally don't like turnip greens by themselves much, but lots of people do. When you mix them with other spring greens, the combination is much better than plain turnip greens, to my taste.

Carrots (*Daucus carota*) are vegetables that have been around for a long time and that are packed with nutrition. The original carrots were white or yellow and originated in modern-day Afghanistan. As the carrot evolved from a bitter white-rooted plant through purple, yellow, and orange roots that became increasingly sweet and large, it moved about the world. Today we find white, yellow, orange, violet, and purple varieties growing wherever gardeners are at work. Not only can you choose color, but you can also select shape. Heirloom carrots come in a variety of sizes from small balls to long tapers, with everything in between.

Beets (*Beta vulgaris* var. *conditiva*) are my personal favorite among the root crops. They are beautiful and tasty, and I like both the root and the leaves. Members of the beet family, which includes chard and sugar beets, are all packed with nutrients, are versatile in the kitchen, and taste good. The ancient Greeks and Romans grew both red and white varieties of table beets as well as what we call Swiss chard.

Natives of the Mediterranean area originally enjoyed beet leaves on the dinner tables, and the roots were used as medicine. Gradually, both parts of the plant became popular foods. Outside the United States, beets are generally referred to as "beetroot."

One of the most widely grown beets is Detroit Dark Red. Introduced into trade in 1892, this beet is almost perfectly globe shaped, delicious, and a good keeper. Another great heirloom is Chioggia, introduced to American gardeners in the late 1840s from Italy. This beautiful beet has alternating red and white concentric rings that resemble a bull's eye. If you want to preserve the pattern, bake your beet whole as you would a potato and slice it crossways. Gold and white heirloom varieties are also available. All have delicious tender greens.

Two things all root crops have in common are that they are better if you grow them yourself than if you buy them at the store, and they require good soil of some depth in which to grow. Since they grow underground, the soil has to be loose enough to let them expand and flourish. Before planting your root crops, dig the bed thoroughly and remove as many rocks as you can. Add a good measure of compost, since root crops are all fairly heavy feeders, and let the bed rest a while before planting. A few years ago I had trouble getting my beet seeds to germinate. One of my readers recommended adding epsom salts to the soil at planting. I don't know why, but that solved the problem. All of these crops are tough enough to withstand light frosts, so get the seeds in the ground early enough so that the plants can mature before the weather gets really hot. In the South, all of these root vegetables can be grown in both spring and fall gardens.

Turnips and beets can be thinned and the greens eaten in delightful early spring salads or cooked quickly and seasoned with salt, pepper, and butter. Space all your seedlings so they have room to grow, and make sure they have enough water to keep them growing steadily. All these crops prefer cool weather. In the South they are terrific in the fall garden and mature throughout the winter. In areas where the soil doesn't freeze, they can stay in the garden until you are ready to eat them. In colder areas, remove them from the soil and store them in a cool place. A root cellar is perfect, but a garage works well in most places.

Regular spraying with a blend of seaweed and fish emulsion keeps your plants healthy and growing quickly. Adding more compost as top dressing never hurts. Too much nitrogen fertilizer will discourage root growth, so stay away from that. Interplant your roots with each other to confuse the bugs. A few onions and garlic mixed in will add another deterrent factor.

Each of these vegetables is delicious on its own as a side dish, but they are also essential ingredients in many wonderful soups, casseroles, and other tasty treats. Once you learn the joys of root crops, you'll wonder how you ever had a garden without them.

Winter Vegetable Soup

2 Tbsp. butter
2 cups chopped leeks (white and some of the green)
1 tsp. minced garlic
1 cup thinly sliced carrots
1 cup thinly sliced turnips
1 cup thinly sliced celery
8 cups broth—chicken, beef, vegetable or a mix of all three
½ cup small pasta
Salt and pepper
2 Tbsp. chopped parsley

Heat butter and cook the leeks until wilted (5–10 minutes) over
   medium heat. Add the garlic and cook for a minute.
Add other vegetables and broth. Bring to a boil, reduce heat, and
   cook gently 20 minutes or so.
Stir in the pasta and herbs and season with salt and pepper. Cook
   until pasta is done and serve with grated cheese. You can add any
   other veggies you have around to this basic soup and substitute
   rice or barley for the pasta (cook them first). You can add beets
   to the soup if you don't mind everything turning maroon or if
   you use a beet that isn't dark colored.

Easter Eggs and Pickled Beets

An easy way to dye eggs for the Easter table is by combining them
with pickled beets

6 cups sliced, cooked beets
12 hard-boiled eggs, peeled
2 cups water
1½ cups vinegar
1 cup sugar
1 cinnamon stick
10 whole cloves
4 whole allspice

Place the beets and eggs in a large glass or ceramic jar or bowl. Combine the remaining ingredients and cook over low heat until everything is combined and smells really good. Pour over the beets and eggs and refrigerate for at least one day before serving. The eggs will turn a beautiful beet red and everything will taste delicious. To obtain a different look, don't peel the eggs, just crack them. Store in the fridge for two days and the resulting eggs will have a marbled look. You can make deviled eggs with a pink outer edge for Easter dinner.

Crisp Winter Salad

Grate turnips, beets, and carrots. Slice leeks thinly. (Use enough to feed your family at one meal.) Toss everything with minced fresh parsley and your favorite vinaigrette dressing. Serve on a bed of shredded red cabbage, and your family will be delighted. If you don't have a favorite vinaigrette, here's mine:

½ cup olive oil
¼ cup safflower oil
¼ cup fresh lemon juice
Salt and pepper to taste
1 tsp. dry mustard

Whisk and then pour into a jar with a tight lid. Shake well and pour enough to moisten the salad. Store the rest in the fridge and use whenever you need a good basic salad dressing.

Sentimental Favorites: Flowers

Roses

Of all the heirloom plants around, probably old roses are the most beloved. They have been appreciated for a very long time. Ancestors of modern roses were found to have been growing in British Columbia forty-five million to fifty million years ago. The Chinese cultivated roses in their gardens five thousand years ago. In 300 BC people were cultivating and selling natural hybrid roses formed by cross-pollination by bees or other insects.

In Shakespeare's day roses were used to add aroma to food, drink, even toothpaste. Roses perfumed soaps, scented the air, and flavored medicines. Wine and jelly and syrup were made of rose petals. Nuns and other devout women cooked up rose petals and made beads that were then made into rosaries, hence the name. When the beads were passed through the hands, they released a sweet and subtle scent.

In the western world we have been breeding new roses for more than a hundred years. You can imagine how many roses that adds up to. And you can also see why many varieties have been lost along the way. In 1867 the first hybrid tea roses were developed. The hybrid teas made big, beautiful flowers and became all the rage. Old-fashioned roses were forgotten in the race to new colors and showy blossoms. The emphasis in the rose growing trade was on hybrid teas and on growing flowers for flower shows. It didn't really matter what the bush looked like as long as the blossoms were impressive.

In the early 1980s, however, people began to notice that the old roses had some really desirable characteristics and the hybrid teas had some real disadvantages. Now the pendulum has swung back and people are once again interested in antique and old garden roses. These plants are not specimen flowers. They look good in the yard even when they aren't

blooming. They are easy to grow, and they can be grown on their own roots, making them much hardier than grafted roses. An antique rose is defined as a variety that is more than fifty years old. Remember that almost all roses are hybrids, but these are often natural hybrids, or they are ones that have proven themselves able to keep producing and growing in spite of bad conditions.

By the time the pendulum swung back to old roses, very few were being offered by nurseries and rose growers. Discovering the old roses became a challenge. Many were found in old neighborhoods, in graveyards, and in the country around abandoned farmsteads. These were roses that could look after themselves, and people decided that was a good thing. As the roses were collected, they were compared with old rose catalogs, and their original names were found. A few had been known throughout the whole period.

People grow old roses for two main reasons: practicality and romance. Old roses are practical because

1. They are easy to grow, require no spraying and little care.
2. They are good in the landscape. They make attractive plants that blend well with other plants.
3. They are pretty, whether in the yard or in a vase.
4. They are versatile; you can select from a wide variety of colors, shapes, and sizes. You can use them as hedges, fences, accent plants, and container plants.

The romance of old roses is easy to understand. They are living antiques, having been passed down from generation to generation as treasured heirlooms. Many roses have a connection with history. For example, the Louis Philippe rose was brought to Texas in 1838 by Francisco de Zavala, who was ambassador to France from the Republic of Texas. Growing here since that time, it is still a beautiful and tough little red rose. And old roses often have a connection to special people in our lives. Roses are passed from friend to friend or from family member to family member. I have a rose that grew on my mother's back trellis for years and years. When I moved I took a cutting, which I have passed on to friends and family. My mother and the original rose are gone, but the feelings and memories are still there. I hate to admit it but often when I pass that rose in bloom, I talk to it and feel closer to my mother just knowing that it was her rose.

So those are the good reasons to grow old roses, but what roses should you grow? Roses, just as every other plant in the world, have a preference for climate. Some roses will survive and thrive in hot climates, while others prefer cooler regions. So be careful when you read an article in a magazine recommending old varieties; make sure they are talking about roses that grow where you live.

There are many misconceptions about old roses. Here are a few:

1. They all have tiny flowers.
2. Their flowers are all single blooms.
3. They are all climbers—viney, ramblers.
4. They bloom only once a year.
5. They grow wild and don't need any care at all.
6. They don't get black spot or any other problem.
7. They are not hybrid; they are "wild."
8. They are all alike.

All of these things are true of some roses, but none are true of all old roses. In fact, there is much diversity in old roses: types, shapes, colors, sizes, growth patterns. Some have powerful thorns, some have almost none. Some have huge flowers, some have tiny ones. It all depends on the rose.

China roses are the only naturally reblooming roses. As their name implies, these roses were found growing in China and were brought to Europe and bred with existing roses to create almost all the everblooming varieties. If it reblooms, it's probably got some China rose in its background. Some examples are Mutabilis, Old Blush, Martha Gonzales, Archduke Charles, Ducher, and that Louis Philippe that de Zavala brought from France. Characteristics of China roses are delicate flowers; pointy leaves; sweet, fruity fragrance; and constant bloom. These roses tolerate alkaline and clay soils without missing a beat, and they can stand lots of heat and humidity. China roses also have a tendency to change colors. Mutabilis goes from yellow to red, Archduke Charles goes from pink to red, and others have less noticeable changes.

China roses start blooming early and keep on blooming until the first freeze. I have a wonderful Mutabilis bush that came to me as proof of the toughness of old roses. I found it growing in a one-gallon pot at the Gabriel Valley Farms nursery of my friends Sam and Cathy Slaughter. They had decided not to grow roses, and this one had been forgotten in the back of a field. The roots had grown through the bottom of the plastic pot, through the weed-blocking ground cover, and into the rocky soil below. When I pulled up the pot, a root about the size of a broom handle broke off. I took the rose home, cut it out of the pot, and planted it on the side of the house next to the street.

For a while it looked awful. The leaves all wilted and then fell off. I watered it with seaweed to try to minimize the shock, but that was a big root I'd broken off. I didn't have a lot of faith, but I did have hope. I kept watering, and before long some new leaves appeared. That was three years ago. Today that rose bush is about 8 feet wide and 7 feet tall. It blooms all the time and gets very little care. That side of the house rarely gets additional water. The roses get some fertilizer in the spring, and that's all. In spite of being generally ignored, this rose bush causes people to stop their car and ask its name. It is so beautiful with its yellow, peachy, pink, and crimson flowers that it almost takes your breath away.

Tea roses are not to be confused with hybrid teas. The old tea roses were the basis of the hybrid teas because they have lovely pointed buds and a perfect rose look. They form chunky V-shaped shrubs, often with

reddish new foliage. They are called tea roses because their scent reminds some people of tea. These roses are the backbone of warm-climate gardens. They are sometimes slow to get started, but they will last for generations and produce beautiful blooms that make excellent cut flowers. Some examples of these roses are Mrs. Dudley Cross, which is virtually thornless; Sombrueil, which is a gorgeous white climber; and Mrs. B. R. Cant, which makes a huge bush covered with beautiful pink flowers. My Mrs. Dudley Cross is a favorite for several reasons. The main one, of course, is that it blooms continuously from frost to frost. And then the yellow blossoms with pink accents remind me of a fresh-faced little girl who has gotten into her mother's lipstick: a dab of pink here, a smear of pink there.

Bourbon roses were named for the Isle of Bourbon (now called Réunion), where they were naturally hybridized. The Bourbons produce beautiful flowers that are large, full, and wonderfully scented. They smell rich and sweet—just like you think a rose ought to smell. They also bloom often in spite of hot weather. Examples of this class are Souvenir de la Malmaison, Zepherine Drouhin, and Maggie. Zepherine is a thornless climber, and Maggie is one of the most prolific bloomers around. Both have bright pink red-flowers.

Hybrid musk is a category of bushes that are long-caned and usually either climbers or arching shrubs. They produce flowers in clusters and can tolerate a little more shade than other groups. Penelope, Nanae, Felicia, Will Scarlet, and Buff Beauty are examples of this group.

Found roses are old roses that have been found growing but cannot be given their old name because nobody knows it. Such roses as Martha Gonzales, Highway 290 Pink Buttons, and Georgetown Tea are all examples of the tough old roses that keep on blooming and growing with or without their original name. In the past few years growers have identified the found rose named Katy Road Pink as the original Carefree Beauty. Still, diehard old rose lovers still refer to it as Katy Road or "the rose formerly known as Katy Road."

Other roses known as antiques or old roses are easy to grow in varying degrees. Miniatures are very easy to grow, almost never have disease or pest problems, and bloom vigorously. Sometimes there is a difference between nursery minis and grocery store minis. Grocery store minis are often grown to be decorative and then thrown out—they are like cut flowers. Sometimes they will grow and do very well in the garden; sometimes they don't. Minis grown for the nursery trade are vigorous and easy to grow.

Noisette is another group that I particularly like. These are often climbers and have beautiful big flowers. Crepuscule, Maracel Neil, and others are in that group. Species roses, gallica, damask, centifolia, moss, perpetuals, polyantha, and floribunda roses don't do as well in my garden as they do in cooler climates, although you might get one that is just fine. There are no absolutes in gardening.

Selecting old roses is one of the hardest jobs I know. I want one of each! But it is also the most fun. It is easy to grow roses using organic methods. Don't fall for that old story about how you have to "spray" your roses. You can rely on them doing well if you follow a few simple rules.

1. Plant in a sunny spot; roses need at least six hours of sun a day.
2. Allow for air circulation. Fungi love dead air.
3. Enrich the soil. Old roses will live in poor soil, but they will bloom more generously and be more beautiful when the soil is improved. Before you plant your rose, enrich the soil with about one-third compost. Mulch over the top of the soil will discourage weeds and keep the soil moist. Compost is the best mulch, but any natural material will work.
4. Feed at least twice a year. Use a foliar feed more often—seaweed and fish is good. The rose food I buy is a nice combination of the nutrients roses love, such as alfalfa and molasses.
5. Water well at least until well established. Although old roses are drought tolerant when they are established, any new plant needs water while its roots are growing and reaching out.

Roses, like all flowering plants, will bloom more if you pinch off the spent blossoms. Contrary to what you might have read, you don't have to do some complicated leaf counting system—just pinch off their heads! It's good for them and good for you, too. I love to deadhead. I can get out my frustrations that way.

Finally, enjoy those roses. They are the queens of the garden, the subject of poets, and they are more fun than anything!

Annuals

When my kids were little we drove fairly regularly from our house in Austin to my mother's house in Sherman, a trip of about two hundred miles. Many times we left after school and didn't get there until it was completely dark. On some of those occasions Mother, who was very security minded, locked the screen door so my key wouldn't let us in, turned off the back porch light, and went upstairs to her bedroom. That left us standing on the back porch yelling and pounding trying to get in. (Those were the days before cell phones.) I remember one time when I was stomping around on the concrete porch trying to get in or get her attention when I stumbled over a large clump of flowers. "What a stupid place to put a flower pot!" I thought and continued my efforts to get into the house.

The next morning when I went out the back door, I was amazed to see a huge clump of old-fashioned petunias growing in the middle of the concrete porch. They had come up in a hairline crack in the pavement and had flourished. I liked those petunias well enough before that, but I have loved them ever since. They were beautiful flowers that ranged from white to almost purple blooms with every hue in between.

I took home some plants from my mother's house, and they grew for a few years, but I lost them. Since then I've found more at local nurseries and paid better attention. I find that unlike many hybrid petunias, these often last two or three years. They also reseed, creating new plants fairly readily. They continue to bloom even when the weather is very hot, something I can never make hybrid petunias do no matter what the label says. They have a nice, sweet fragrance and serve well both as container plants and in the garden.

Although not easy to find, old-fashioned petunias are worth the search. Some catalogs call them "Petunia multiflora—old fashioned vining petunia." I'm told that in some places they have escaped cultivation and become local wildflowers. I wish they would here!

Another wonderful reseeding annual is the old golden yellow cosmos (*Cosmos bipinnatus*). I've not had a lot of luck with the pretty pink and purple cosmos, but these yellow orange ones have their own big life going on in my front yard. The ugly truth of the matter is that I pay a lot

of attention to my vegetable beds and almost no attention to the other things in my garden. I don't water much, don't fertilize much, and once something seems happy there, I leave it alone. These cosmos seem to delight in being left alone.

I stuck in some bedding plants about four years ago, and they've been reseeding, blooming, and impressing strangers ever since. I've sold seeds, given away seeds, potted up young plants, whacked them down with abandon when they got too tall, and I still have a bed full of these cheerful bloomers. Some came up down the street in a neighbor's yard. If we didn't have pretty good pavement in the street, I expect they would sprout there. These are wonderful, self-sufficient plants that are pretty outside and great cut flowers as well.

When I think of heirloom annuals, the first flower I think of is zinnia. When I was a little girl, my daddy dug up a little flower bed for me in the backyard, and I planted zinnias (*Zinnia*). They are so easy and so pretty I think more people should grow them. I think the reason more gardeners don't have zinnias is because they are thought of as a sort of "common" flower. There is really nothing groovy or grand about zinnias. Native to Mexico, the original zinnias were small, weedy looking plants with a dull purple bloom. Although the Spanish thought them "eyesores," they took some seeds home, and botanists went to work. By the 1700s they had succeeded in turning the humble original zinnias into a beautiful garden flower.

Zinnias are easy to grow from seed, and the seeds are easy to save from year to year. When you find a flower you particularly like, let it dry on the plant, then pull it off and save the seeds for next year. The biggest problem with zinnias is that their foliage is very susceptible to fungi. Water on the leaves makes them turn white and brown and dead looking. The solution, of course, is never to get water on the leaves, but who's going to do that? If I can get the sprinkler out and running during the dog days of summer, I've done my part. I don't have drip irrigation, and I'm not going to stand there making sure I don't get water on the zinnias' leaves. So I live with a little fungus and don't worry about it. The flowers are still great looking—bright and cheerful outside and a sure sign of summer's bounty indoors.

I went through a period of thinking annuals were too pedestrian. All those public plantings of masses of petunias, begonias, and other annuals that looked just alike and could as easily have been plastic made me a snob. Then I realized what I was missing. Annuals are the highlight of the summer garden. They add bright colors and wonderful smells and provide beauty for the inside of the house as well.

Now that I've come to my senses, I can't wait to put out seeds and young plants in the spring. Sweet peas (*Lathyrus odoratus*) provide very early beauty and fragrance; bachelor buttons (*Centaurea cyanus*) remind me of my youth; larkspurs (*Delphinium*) are the most regal and gorgeous plants I know, and the list goes on and on. Now I don't look down my nose at old-fashioned annuals; I get down on my knees and scratch them into yet another corner of the garden. I stick them in the vegetable beds when crops are done, put them in pots to sit on the sunny porch, and take bouquets to friends whether they want them or not.

Perennials

I do love flowers, and I particularly love flowers that can be brought into the house. I can't imagine a garden without flowers, either annual or perennial, and I prefer to have some of both.

Heirloom perennials share one of the best traits of old roses. They are wonderful reminders of old times and old friends. I have bought very few of the perennials that grow in my garden. Most were gifts, and I like to think of them as love gifts. Nothing, in my opinion, shows love better than a living gift of plants.

Of course, there are also some wonderful plants available for purchase. Check around at local plant fairs to see if you can find something old and interesting that you haven't grown before. At a Master Gardener conference I found a man selling beautiful red oxblood lily bulbs (*Rhodophiala bifida*). I'd always wanted some of those and had seen them growing in strangers' gardens, but my friends were inconsiderate enough not to have any. I snapped up some bulbs and put them in the garden. They make fall so much more colorful.

Perennials can give you beauty all year around. The bulbs and irises start blooming in my garden in late winter and take me through until late spring, when the main-season flowers start. Those go until fall bloomers begin, and the cycle begins again.

The first to bloom in my garden are some bulbs that came from my friends the Hickses. I've known Mike and Kathryn since we were kids in school, but I didn't know until too late that Mike's mother was a big-time bearded iris collector (*Iris germanica*). She had a huge number of exotic varieties in her garden that she had collected wherever she went. By the time I found out, however, she'd been gone for a while, and all that remained were the really good, really tough, really old varieties of irises. Mike and Kathryn shared those with me.

We met in Chandler at Blue Moon Gardens one lovely spring day, and in the back of their car was a big tangle of bulbs, roots, leaves, and dirt. The tangle was transferred to the back of my car, and my new garden was off and running. I planted the irises, daffodils, and other mystery bulbs and waited with bated breath until the next spring. I was not disappointed; the flowers were beautiful and looked wonderful in my

constantly evolving landscape. And year after year I think of the Hickses when the bulbs bloom and I am glad of their friendship, of his mother's enthusiasm, and of the portability of great old plants.

In addition to the Hicks irises, I have irises that grew in my mother's garden that I dug up shortly before turning over her house to strangers. These deep purple beauties don't bloom every year, but when they do, they are dramatic and glorious. I also have yellow irises from a fellow gardener who drove up my driveway; dumped a clump of rhizomes in the yard; said, "Here! These are taking over my yard!" and drove away. They are quite tough and will gladly fill a space.

Another clump of perennial bulbs came from an old home where we attended an estate sale. The people were selling their parents' house and lived far away. "We can't take any of these," they said, "but you are welcome to them." I didn't know those people or their parents, but I'm happy to have the bulbs, and they continue a tradition of passalong plants that make gardeners a happy band willing to share their goodies with each other.

I am much more interested in having interesting plants and plants that make me happy than in having an orderly landscape. That might be a personality flaw, but it is one I can live with, so I almost never turn down a plant. My philosophy is that if a plant does well in my garden, it is welcome there. If it doesn't, it is welcome in the compost heap.

A few years ago a friend gave me a pot of flowers she didn't know the name of. It was pretty, she said, and easy to grow. That plant sat in the pot in the garden all summer and never bloomed. The next year I found samples of that plant all over the place. Apparently it snuck out of the hole in the bottom of the pot and sent root runners all through the grass, into the vegetable beds, and up and down the border. I learned that this plant is *Clerodendrum bungei,* also known as cashmere bouquet plant, Mexicali rose, Mexican hydrangea, and rose glory bower. It is a pretty flower that attracts butterflies and has a nice scent, but in my garden it is a rampant weed. It demands too much water or looks like a wilted stick. It comes up everywhere and takes up too much room. It only blooms when it is soaked, and those @#$%& underground runners make it ridiculously invasive. Maybe in areas where it gets cold and freezes down or where it rains a lot it would be welcome, but not here. To add insult to injury, ants love it and will gather for parties around its stems. So I've been working on murdering it ever since.

This cautionary tale is to encourage you to find out about the plants you are generously offered by friends before you introduce them to your garden. Better yet, try to see them growing in another garden before moving them to yours.

One of my very favorite plants that I've moved from one place to another is the Shasta daisy (*Leucanthemum maximum*) that grew in my mother's garden and has grown in my various gardens since. No flower is more cheery than the white daisy with a yellow center. After all, what else can be "fresh as a daisy"? Shasta and ox-eye daisies (*L. vulgare*) are the classic white and yellow flowers, and they are easily confused and also

easily grown side-by-side. In fact, if you grow both, you'll have daisies in the garden for a longer period of time, since the Shastas start earlier and end earlier than the ox-eyes.

I dug up my first clump of daisies from my mother's garden roughly thirty years ago. The clump expands and is easily divided to make more. I've purchased more, planted some seeds, and don't actually know which ones came from mother's house, but that's okay. I prefer to think they all did. I love the flowers, and I enjoy remembering her nice, shady yard where they and I grew.

In spite of their apparent innocence and cheerfulness, daisies have been credited with the ability to foretell the future, particularly with regard to love. We've all picked daisy petals to determine whether he loves me or not. Closing your eyes and picking a handful of daisies is supposed to reveal the number of years left before you find your true love—a belief that will make the picker grab a small handful even if the eyes are closed. If you want to actually see that dream person—in a dream—just put a daisy root under your pillow before bedtime.

Daisies like rich soil with bright light. Adding compost, well-rotted manure, and some minerals to the soil before planting is a good idea, because those plants are going to be there for a long time. Water well while they are getting established and when they are forming blossoms. Pests don't seem interested in daisies, another great thing about them.

I have other mementos in my garden that remind me of people daily. There is the well-named mother of millions, or thousands (*Bryophyllum daigremontianum*)—depending on how well your plant grows, I guess— that came from Victor Martin's mother's garden on the Texas Gulf Coast. A woman from the Lady Bird Johnson Wildflower Center in Austin entrusted me with a salvia plant that she assured me was in danger of extinction. I don't know why. It is a big, gorgeous, pushy plant with purple red flowers, and it gets bigger every year. There are pots of begonias of two different types and something else I can't remember the name of flourishing on the front porch and given to me by Margaret Green, an extraordinary gardener who is forever saying she doesn't know how to garden. And there are more. The flowers are just the start of the pleasures these plants give me.

Herbs

When you start talking about old plants, none are older than the plants we call herbs. Useful plants that have been grown and harvested for food, medicine, dyes, scents, and much more, herbs are essential elements in any kitchen or garden. For the most part, herbs are tough and will grow with almost no attention from the gardener. They are often fragrant and help keep pests away from your garden and beneficial insects at work in your garden. Many can turn a boring meal into a taste treat. Others can help you feel better free of charge.

I recommend you grow as many kinds of herbs as you possibly can and enjoy the other ones by buying them fresh from the market. Obviously, I love herbs and wrote a whole book about them to encourage others to love them as well (*What Can I Do With My Herbs?* Texas A&M University Press, 2009), so I'll only mention a few sentimental favorites here.

Mullein

Have you noticed that many of my sentimental favorites have to do with my youth? I guess that makes sense. When we are young, we are constantly discovering new things and learning about them. The world is new and exciting. Later, we develop a ho-hum, oh-yes-I-know-all-about-that attitude. I grew up in an old two-storey house in an old neighborhood. Across the street from our house was another old two-storey frame house surrounded by once-white picket fence. No one lived in that house, but every day three very strange looking old people—two men and one woman—came by, went through the picket gate, and entered the house. A few minutes later they would come out and continue down the sidewalk. They were all short and fairly wide. To me they looked

like gnomes I'd seen in story books. I remember them as always bundled up and wearing overcoats, although they must have worn other clothes. It was Texas, after all, and hot most of the time.

I learned from my mother that those people had grown up in the house, and that since their mother had died the house had become a sort of shrine. Nothing had changed since her death; no stranger had been into the house, and their daily visits consisted of "checking" to make sure everything was okay. More than anything I wanted to go into that house, and more than anything else that house seemed very scary to me. I was sure that the mother's ghost resided there. It was obviously a haunted house and probably the meeting place for witches as well.

One of the creepy elements of the scene was that the yard was filled, not with grass like everyone else's yards, but with big-leafed grey green plants with tall spikes coming out of their centers. In my mind those were spooky plants, related to the spookiness of the house. I don't think my mother knew what those plants were, either, because it was much later that I realized they were mullein (*Verbascum thapsus*).

So I was right. Mullein has long been associated with witchcraft. It was given to Ulysses to protect him from sorcery and has a long history as a protective herb. My guess is that it grew in the garden across the street to protect us from the spooks within and to protect the spooks within from us. (I never got into that house. It burned to the ground from a lightning strike some years later. Oooh!)

Mullein is a biennial plant that readily reseeds in the garden—hence the many plants across the street. The first year it produces big, velvety leaves with fine hairs all over them. The second year it produces a tall stalk of little yellow flowers. These stalks traditionally have been dipped in wax or fat to create long-burning torches. The leaves are used as bandages and during wartime have lined many worn-out shoes.

The roots, leaves, and flowers of the mullein plant have all been used as medicines. A tea made of the leaves (strained through cheesecloth or coffee filters to remove the hairs) is useful in treating sore throats and coughs. It is also said to be good for digestion and as a remedy for allergies. Native Americans also smoked the dried leaves to treat chest congestion and inhaled the steam rising from the tea to soothe a sore throat. This is not a tea you'll drink for pleasure. In my opinion, it tastes like dirty dishwater, although I have never tasted dirty dishwater. Mullein root been used to support urinary tract health and help with bladder control. It is most often used in tinctures.

The bright little yellow flowers that bloom on the top of the stalk are good mixed into a bland cream to smooth dry skin. A more concentrated mix of cream and dried leaves seems to have a drawing effect on boils, pimples, and other sore spots. Soaking the flowers in olive oil for several days will serve as eardrops or as a rub for aching joints. There is a long list of medicinal uses for mullein, but primarily I use it as a garden plant.

Because of its ability to reseed, mullein wanders at will around my garden. It comes up one year in the vegetable bed, another in the flower border. One year it joined the tansy in a big container. Sometimes it sprouts in the lawn, where it is promptly mowed down. It is fun to see where it will appear next. Mullein will grow in bad or good soil, prefers sun to shade but will take some shade, and can take high heat and humidity. Is it any wonder this is a favorite plant of people both dead and alive?

Comfrey

An herb that looks something like mullein is comfrey (*Symphytum officinale*). Both plants have large rosettes of wide leaves that grow close to the ground, but whereas mullein sends up a tall stalk, comfrey produces a short stalk of delicate flowers that are white, lavender, or pink bell-like blossoms.

Comfrey was brought to Europe by Crusaders who found it growing in the Middle East and learned of its amazing healing powers. Once considered a miracle worker, comfrey was known as knitbone because it was able to stimulate the healing of broken bones and many other wounds of war. Comfrey leaves contain a substance called allantoin, which is a natural chemical compound with hormonelike properties that stimulate cell growth. This characteristic helps repair and heal wounds, broken bones, burns, sprains, sore joints, dry skin, and swelling. Most commonly, people make a poultice of chopped comfrey leaves wrapped in damp cheesecloth and apply it to the wound. Soaking the cloth in comfrey tea doubles the effect. You can also make a soothing cream by mixing dried and crumbled or chopped fresh comfrey leaves into a bland base such as calendula cream. You can also buy comfrey cream at health food stores. It has been used for a variety of problems, including ringworm, poison ivy, and sprains. Simply wrapping a sore finger in a comfrey leaf when working in the garden may get the healing process started quickly.

Comfrey has been used this way for generations. Be sure, however, before you use a lot of it that you are not allergic to it. Apply a small amount to a spot on your skin and watch it for a couple of days. Comfrey should not be taken internally because of the high concentration of alkaloids it contains, but folk medicine strongly believes in its topical effects.

Comfrey is also a beneficial plant in the garden. Because it has a deep tap root (as much as 10 feet), it is able to reach deep into the soil. The expansion of roots loosens the soil and lets beneficial microbes and earthworms work on the health of the soil.

The leaves of comfrey contain calcium; potassium; phosphorus; vitamins A, C, and B12; and other nutrients. The concentration of these elements in the plant can be used to feed the soil. Comfrey makes a big mounding clump of large leaves that quickly replenish themselves when they are cut. You can use those leaves in the compost heap, as mulch for neighboring plants, or to make liquid fertilizer.

Comfrey is a lovely garden plant as well. It grows 2 to 2½ feet tall and about the same width. The flowers appear in the spring and intermittently throughout the growing season. It grows from root divisions, so it is easy to share with friends or to create new plants. Only a small piece of root is needed to start a new clump. Keep it watered until it is established and then it becomes fairly drought tolerant. It is happy in full sun or partial shade and is tolerant of poor soil and even damp soil. In cold weather the plant will die to the ground and then reemerge in the spring. When winters are mild, many of the leaves will remain evergreen.

Rosemary

If you are looking for an evergreen herb, a plant that can withstand relentless sun and heat, or a plant that provides wonderful aromas in the garden and tastes in the house, or maybe one you can trim into a fancy topiary, you can't do better than rosemary. Rosemary is versatile, tough, beautiful, and tasty. Besides all that, it is good for you and a great addition to the home and garden in a wide variety of ways.

Rosemary (*Rosemarinus officinalis*) is an ancient herb that originated in the Mediterranean area and was gathered in the wild and used by the ancient Romans and Greeks for fragrance, medicine, and magic. Rosemary contains a substance called carnosic acid, a potent antioxidant that is being studied as useful in maintaining a healthy brain. It also is one of the few antioxidants that is "slow release," becoming available not only immediately after ingestion but for a long time afterwards.

It is interesting how many times folklore, folk medicine, and old wives' tales are proven true by science. For centuries rosemary has been associated with memory and the mind. Shakespeare talked about it, and it came down to him from aeons past. Now modern research is proving that indeed rosemary stimulates the brain and keeps it healthy. It has been said that one way rosemary supports the brain function is by strengthening the circulatory system, which is helpful for the whole body as well as the brain.

Rosemary likes plenty of sun and hates being damp. It needs really good drainage, so if you are growing it in a container, add coarse sand or pebbles to your potting soil. If possible, it is much happier growing in the ground. Upright rosemary can grow into a large shrubby bush, and several will make a great hedge in a sunny spot. Prostrate rosemary grows nicely on a hill, tumbling down and creating good erosion control as well as a nice landscape. If you have a spot with lots of sun and poor, rocky soil, rosemary will be very happy there. In temperate climates rosemary will be evergreen. In cold areas it needs to be brought indoors for the winter. Very cold weather will kill the plant.

I have one acquaintance who talks about her "pet" rosemary plant. It grows just outside the back door, and whenever she walks outside she gives it a friendly pat on the "head." That pat releases some of the great rosemary scent and makes her feel cheerful for simply passing by. It is almost impossible to walk by a rosemary bush without running your hands through it. Nothing smells better or scents your hand with a nicer lingering odor.

That is one of the reasons that rosemary makes such a great plant to bring indoors. Of course it is a wonderful plant to decorate with at Christmas because it looks like traditional pine boughs but smells much better. You can use it for wreaths, topiary trees, and garlands. But don't limit its use to the holidays. A sprig of rosemary in the clothes closets and linen closets will make things smell fresh at the same time it repels moths and other insect pests. A strong tea of rosemary or rosemary vinegar is perfect for cleaning nonporous surfaces in the house and bathroom, disinfecting as it goes. Simply adding a bouquet of rosemary stems to a vase in any room will freshen the air.

While rosemary is easy to grow if you give it conditions it likes, it also will occasionally suddenly fall over dead. This is a sort of annoying habit, and I'm never sure why it happens, but it does. I'm sure my latest rosemary casualty was a result of overcrowding.

I planted rosemary in a border next to a climbing rose and some other plants. Rosemary needs air circulation to prevent fungal problems, and my rose was more vigorous than I expected. It grew over and around the rosemary, cutting off the sun and air circulation, and one day all the rosemary leaves turned brown and fell off. The same thing has happened when the plant was pruned too severely. Although I've read that you can prune rosemary by half, I don't recommend it. Some rosemary plants go into shock when they are drastically pruned and never recover. The primary reason for sudden death in rosemaries, I'm sure, is poor drainage. Sitting in damp soil will do in a rosemary plant in no time at all.

But don't let all that discourage you. Every home needs a rosemary plant—in the ground or in a container. The piney flavor goes beautifully with many foods—meat, breads, potatoes, beans, and even desserts and drinks. Bees love the flowers and make divine rosemary honey from them. Rosemary tea is soothing, healing, and tasty. It will also make your hair sparkle if you use it as an after-shampoo rinse. Rosemary is a wonderfully versatile herb and enjoyable year-round.

Trees, Vines, Bushes, and Other Stuff

E very kind of plant has heirloom varieties. Although new hybrids come along at a rapid pace, the old trees, vines, bushes, and every other kind of plant keep producing and remain the soul of the garden. No matter what kind of plant you want to add to your landscape, consider the heirlooms. They have so many good characteristics.

Gingko

Gingko biloba trees are known as living fossils because they are so old that all their plant relatives have become extinct. The last of similar plants died out in the Pliocene epoch, more than two and one-half million years ago, but the gingko tree keeps going. It is the only plant

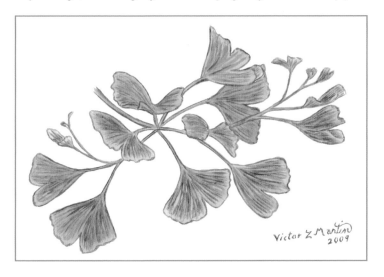

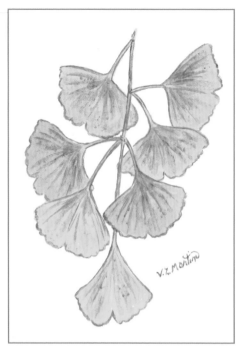

in its biological group. Also called maidenhair tree, this fascinating tree is known to grow in the wild in only two places in China, and there is some debate about whether those groves were planted and maintained over many years by groups of monks. Once common in North America and Europe, gingkos were wiped out by the Ice Age in those areas and disappeared seven million years ago. The trees were thought to be extinct for many years.

These are the oldest living species of tree around and as such are interesting plants. They are also beautiful trees, especially in the fall when the leaves turn a golden yellow and make the whole tree glow. Gingko is a tall tree, sometimes growing more than 150 feet tall but usually stopping at about 80 feet. The leaves are uniquely fan-shaped and flutter nicely in the breeze. There are male and female gingko trees, and the female fruit must be fertilized in order to make a viable seed. Many people think the ripe seeds have a bad smell and purposely plant male trees. The trees can be propagated by seed or cuttings.

Not only is the species an old one, but the trees themselves live a very long time when they are happy where they are planted. Some trees planted at temples in China are more than fifteen hundred years old. Europeans first encountered the trees in Japan in the 1600s and brought back samples. Gingkos have been cultivated in the United States for more than two hundred years.

Gingkos are particularly well suited to urban planting and cope well with pollution and confined spaces. They rarely suffer from diseases, and most insects have no interest in them. Often planted along streets and in areas where soil is poor or scarce, these old trees are the poster child for the toughness of heirlooms plants. The most extreme example of that are the six gingko trees that were growing near the site of the atomic bomb explosion in Hiroshima, Japan, at the end of World War II. Every other living thing in the area was killed, and the ginkgos were charred, but they survived, recovered, and are still alive today.

Many people believe that gingko enhances brain strength, and studies are being done to test that belief. It is said to improve memory and concentration. So far, studies have been inconclusive, and some have found that ginkgo has no effect, but the work continues. In any event, do not go out and eat parts of the tree.

Gingko trees are easy to grow, but you need to be sure to water them well while they are being established. Once established, they are very self-sufficient. Young trees, like many other young things, go through a gangly stage. The foliage is pyramid shaped, and the trees look out of proportion, but in a few years they will grow into stately shade trees and beautiful additions to the landscape. The trees seem to prefer slightly acidic soil but will grow in almost any condition, given a little encouragement. They grow slowly for the first few years, then take off and grow rapidly thereafter. They need full sun and well-draining soil.

Redbud

Whereas gingko tree is old and stately looking, the redbud tree always looks young and fresh. Even old redbuds look young when they dress themselves in pink frills in the early spring. The eastern redbud (*Cercis canadensis*) is a large shrub or small tree native to North America with cousins in Europe and Asia. While the eastern redbud is the most widespread and hardiest of the group, there is also the western or California redbud (*C. occidentalis*) and the Texas redbud (*C. canadensis* var. *texensis*). Eastern redbuds are native to woodlands from Canada to Florida and westward to the Great Plains. Western redbuds are native from southern Utah through California and Arizona. Of course, you know where the Texas variety grows. In Europe and the Mediterranean area, the most common variety is *C. siliquastrum,* often referred to as the Judas tree because of the lore than Judas Iscariot hanged himself from its branches after betraying Jesus.

Native American redbuds have been admired and treasured for centuries for their beauty and usefulness. In fact, the redbud has been nominated as a candidate for national tree by the National Arbor Day Foundation.

Each spring, redbud trees put out dense clusters of bright pink or fuchsia blossoms along their bare, reddish brown trunks and branches. For those of us who grew up with crepe paper flowers, they look a lot like those. But these are real flowers and real beauties. Among the first trees to flower in the spring, redbuds are a harbinger of good things to come. In a generally brown landscape, the bright pink flowers stay on the branches for up to three weeks, adding color to the view and a smile to the faces of passersby. Once the flowers fade, the pretty heart-shaped leaves emerge, and the tree continues to be pretty and cheerful in the landscape. Some varieties have white flowers, if you prefer. I, of course, always go for the gaudy. Because the trees are small in size, they are adaptable to almost any size yard. The eastern redbud grows to 30 feet or less, and the western varieties generally remain 15–20 feet tall.

Rumor has it that either Thomas Jefferson or George Washington gave the redbud its common name. Was either of them colorblind? At any rate, both loved the tree, and the story goes that Washington himself

went into the woods and dug and transplanted dozens of redbuds to his farm at Mount Vernon. They grow at Monticello as well.

Like many wonderful native plants, redbuds are not picky about soil or growing conditions. They will thrive in clay, sand, and any kind of soil as long as there is no standing water. Although members of the legume family, redbuds cannot capture nitrogen from the air as many of their relatives do, but they do produce many bean-looking seed pods. They also can take the heat and cold that is common in their wide range. Redbuds are great understory trees in their native woods, so they can grow beneath large trees in your landscape as well, or they can take full sun if they are the only tree on the block. In addition to all that, redbud trees grow quickly, filling empty spots in no time at all. It is hard to find a more adaptable, easier to enjoy tree.

Redbuds grow easily from seed, so collect some from your favorite tree and give them a try. Pick the seed pods as soon as they begin to dry so the insects and birds don't do it for you; generally there are plenty of seeds for everyone. Let them dry thoroughly and store in a dry spot until you are ready to plant them, preferably in the fall. Because the seeds have a hard covering, they need some treatment before they are planted. You can scarify them by covering them with boiling water and letting them sit overnight, then scratching them with your pocket knife. You can also scarify them by soaking them in high-acid vinegar for a day or two. If you are very brave, you can soak them in sulfuric acid for thirty minutes. Be very careful if you decide to use sulfuric acid. The boiling water method seems to be preferred. After scarifying them, plant your seeds in containers and keep them watered until they sprout. It may take a while, so be patient.

You can, of course, buy young redbud trees at your local nursery or online. In either case, try to get varieties that are best adapted to your area. Young trees need supplemental water until they are established, then they are drought tolerant and easy to grow. General organic fertilizers once a year will encourage growth and bloom, and pruning out any damaged branches will keep your tree beautiful.

Redbuds are not just pretty faces. Traditionally they have been very useful trees as well. Native Americans ate redbud flowers raw or boiled and ate the seeds roasted. Early settlers found the blossoms a delicious and tangy tasting addition to their salads. Native Americans used twigs from the trees to create beautiful and functional baskets and made bows from the larger branches. The roots can be used to create a dark reddish brown dye.

Early folk healers used the bark to treat common maladies and sometimes even leukemia. According to published sources, redbud was mentioned in sixteenth- and seventeenth-century herbals, but none of those sources quote the herbals or tell where they can be found. Native Americans made a tea from the bark to treat whooping cough. Infusions of the bark also treated colds, fever, vomiting, and other common ailments. Tannin boiled from the bark can be used as an antiseptic, disinfectant, and tanning agent for animal skins. The leaves are poisonous, so don't eat them!

People aren't the only ones who enjoy the redbud tree. Birds, deer, caterpillars, squirrels, and other small critters enjoy munching on the seeds and hiding in the branches, but the real redbud lovers in the natural world are bees. All varieties of bees feast on the nectar of the redbud flowers. Because they appear when there is not much more around to enjoy, bees flock to the blossoms. The bees pollinate the flowers during their early spring feast as well. Long-tongued bees like the honeybee, blueberry bee, and carpenter bee pollinate the flowers and make the seeds more abundant and productive.

Susan Wittig Albert, who has written a series of wonderful and popular mysteries about China Bayles, a sleuthing herbalist, offers this recipe for redbud flowers on her website, http://www.abouthyme.com:

Redbud Relish
1½ cups water
4 cups redbud flowers
¾ cup red wine vinegar
1 tsp. coriander seeds
1 tsp. fennel seeds
¼ tsp. ground allspice
¼ tsp. ginger
4 bay leaves

Bring water to a boil and steam the flowers for 15 minutes.
Tie herbs into a cheesecloth bundle. Place flowers in a lidded jar.
Combine vinegar with water used for steaming, add herb bundle, and heat just to boiling. Pour over flowers in a lidded jar. Add herb bundle. Let sit for at least 24 hours before serving.
Keeps in refrigerator for up to 3 months. Use as a garnish with meat, vegetables.

You can also sprinkle redbud flowers on top of your pancakes when you cook them, add them to salads, substitute them for other fruits in fritters, and have fun making up your own recipes.

Gardenia

I can't think of a single plant with a better smell, more beautiful flowers, and more romantic associations than the gardenia (*Gardenia jasmi-
noides*). A bush in full flower is enough to knock most people off their
feet and send them into daydreams of exotic islands complete with hand-
some young men or svelte young women (whichever their preference).

My mother always grew gardenia bushes in the yard and floated the
flowers in a shallow bowl of water on the dining table when they were in
bloom. I can remember even as a kid thinking they were the most gorgeous things I'd ever smelled. She emptied pickle jars around the plants
when the pickles were all gone and occasionally poured some vinegar on
them and watered it in well. Obviously gardenias prefer acid soil; at the
time, however, I attributed it to my mother's occasional gardening peculiarity. (She also hung rags and aluminum pie plates in the fig trees.)

Gardenias have been cultivated in Chinese gardens for well over a
thousand years, but Europeans and Americans have known of them for
only a few hundred years. Discovered by the enthusiastic plant hunters
of the eighteenth century, gardenias were found and sent to America to
an amateur naturalist named Alexander Garden. John Ellis, who provided the plant, named it after Garden, whose plantation, Yeshoe, near
Charleston, South Carolina, was the home of many exotic and new species. The plant loved its new home because South Carolina provided the
hot, humid weather and acidic soil of its native area.

The flowers are a beautiful ivory color, and that, combined with their
scent, made the bush a favorite around the world. It was worn by Billie
Holiday, first as a result of an accident and later as a signature look.
According to Carmen McRae, Holiday burned her hair with a curling
iron when those irons were heated on a stove and got very hot. She was
panicked, not wanting to go on stage with a hole in her hair. Someone
ran out looking for flowers and found a street vendor selling gardenias,
and Holiday put some in her hair to cover the burned spot. She liked the
flower and the look so well that she wore gardenias in her hair for many
years afterward.

In the Victorian language of flowers, gardenias represented joy, and it
is joyful indeed to find yourself presented with a lovely fragrant gardenia.

When I was a girl we had a lot of formal dances for which the boys brought corsages and the girls boutonnieres. It was always a treat when I found a gardenia in the cellophane-topped box. We knew the boy was a good one if he brought a gardenia and a cheapskate if he brought a carnation. Of course the boy who brought an orchid got the highest marks, but that was pure snobbery. And, oh lord! those wrist corsages. But that's another story.

Part of the feeling of preciousness about gardenias is their fleeting beauty. Touch the petals and they turn brown. Cut them and they last only a few days in a bowl of water. On the shrub they last a bit longer, but they never last long enough. The fragrance makes you want to lean back and wallow in it.

If you are lucky enough to have a spot where gardenias are happy to grow, you are lucky indeed. They prefer slightly acidic soil, morning sun, and a steady supply of water that doesn't get on their leaves. Water on the leaves encourages fungal growth. They are hardy outdoors at least in zone 8 and in cooler zones if well protected. They like hot, humid weather but bloom in the spring before the weather gets extremely hot. Plant in good soil and mulch with an acid material such as oak leaves and coffee grounds. Let the top inch of soil dry out before watering again at the base of the plant. It is possible to grow gardenias in a container, and in that case you can more easily control the acidity of the soil. On the other hand, they will never grow into the tall, fat, prolifically blooming bushes in containers that they do in some soil. Experiment and see what works for you.

If you know someone with lovely gardenia bushes that thrive and bloom well, ask to take cuttings. You can take cuttings of gardenias just as you do roses. Select a pencil-sized stem with leaves growing well on the end. Remove all but the top leaves and stick the stem into a pot of good potting soil. Keep the soil moist and put the pot in a bright location. Avoid full sun, because the leaves will burn. Watch for new growth and transplant to a larger plant once the cuttings start growing.

Plant your gardenias near where you walk or sit outdoors, and be sure to bring some flowers indoors. The blossoms are beautiful, but their scent is heavenly and enough to cheer up the gloomiest day.

Pomegranate

Recently the pomegranate has made an appearance on the fabulous food fad list, being touted as the latest, greatest superfruit. Everywhere you look you see pomegranate juice, syrup, dressing, seeds, and recipes for exotic dishes such as goose with pomegranate glaze and other taste treats. But pomegranates are no new treat. The pomegranate (*Punica granatum*) is an ancient fruit that was featured in Egyptian mythology and art and praised in the Old Testament and the Babylonian Talmud. The plant is native from Iran to the Himalayas in northern India and has been cultivated since ancient times. It has traveled with explorers and settlers around the world and become naturalized in many temperate regions. A naturalized grove was first recorded in Bermuda in 1621. It was introduced in California by Spanish settlers in 1769, and there are many commercial groves there and in Arizona, where the tree enjoys the warm, dry climate.

In ancient times the pomegranate was considered to be among the most valuable of ornamental and medicinal plants. The seeds were supposed to be a symbol of fertility, and one legend opines that the pomegranate was the "tree of life" in the Garden of Eden.

The pomegranate is a large shrub or small tree that can grow up to 30 feet tall. It has many branches and is hard to train as a single-stemmed tree. Dwarf varieties are available (*P. granatum* var. *nana*), and they are widely grown in pots. Dwarf plants produce dwarf fruit. The trees live a long time and are very easy and sturdy. You'll see them planted in public parks and commercial landscapes because they require little or no care. The shiny evergreen leaves make the pomegranate a good-looking landscape plant even when it is not producing flowers or fruit. When it does produce, however, it is gorgeous. The bright orange red flowers are showy and look nice on the bush or in a vase in the house. Following the flowers, the fruit appears and is round with a tough, leathery skin. The interior is separated by spongy white membranes, and the goodness is in the seeds and the liquid sacs that surround them. Pomegranates are not easy or tidy to eat. The process involves a lot of smacking, sucking, and spitting to get the true goodness out of the fruit. I suggest if you want to

Victor Z. Martin
2006

really enjoy eating a pomegranate you take Cactus Pryor's advice about eating tacos: "Do it naked in the shower."

On the other hand, extracting the juice from the fruit is easy and relatively neat. You can cut the fruit in half and use an orange juicer or reamer to get out the juice. If you are looking for a more exotic experience, you could try the Iranian method of wearing special shoes to stomp cut-open fruit in a clay tub. You can probably find pomegranate stomping shoes on the internet.

The juice can be made into jelly or used in recipes or simply enjoyed as is. It has been made into grenadine and used in mixed drinks for years. The juice contains many minerals and some vitamins and is low in calories and high in taste.

Pomegranate Jelly with Ginger

2 cups fresh pomegranate juice (about 4 large pomegranates)
4 cups sugar
1 Tbsp. finely shredded fresh ginger root
¼ tsp. butter
1 to 2 pouches (3 oz. each) liquid pectin (increase pectin for
  firmer jelly)

Add 1 tablespoon finely shredded fresh ginger root to pomegranate juice before cooking. Add juice mixture to a 5 quart nonreac-
  tive saucepan; stir in sugar. Add butter (helps reduce foaming).
Stirring constantly, bring mixture to a full boil over high heat
Quickly stir in pectin. Return to a full boil; boil exactly 1 minute.
Remove from heat; skim off any foam. Immediately pour into hot,
  sterilized canning jars within 1/8 inch of the top; cover with hot,
  sterilized lids. Cool, then refrigerate. To make jelly shelf-stable,
  process filled canning jars according to instructions from jar
  manufacturer. Makes 5 cups.

Pomegranate Margaritas

2 cups pomegranate juice—to fill 1 ice tray
½ cup lime juice
2 Tbsp. orange-flavored liqueur
½ cup tequila

Pour pomegranate juice into ice cube tray. Freeze until solid,
  about 2 hours.
Pop cubes from tray. In a blender combine lime juice, liqueur, and
  tequila. Turn blender to the highest speed and gradually drop in
  all but 2 juice cubes, whirling until slushy.
Wet the top of serving glass and rim with salt. Place a pomegranate cube in the bottom of each glass. Pour margarita mixture in
  and enjoy. Serves 2.

Pomegranate juice is expensive, as are the fruits when you buy them at the grocery store. So growing your own makes good sense. Pomegranates prefer a sunny location and deep soil. They grow as far north as Washington, D.C., in the United States, but they prefer warmer climates. In some areas of the Gulf Coast states they have escaped cultivation and become naturalized.

They can tolerate acid or alkaline soils or any others in between. They will grow in heavy clay as long as there is good drainage. They are drought tolerant and of little interest to insects. You can start a pomegranate tree from either seed or cuttings. According to William Welch of Texas A&M University, "During the winter dormant period 8–10" cuttings may be stuck in containers of potting soil or directly into well prepared beds in the garden." You can also simply toss an old pomegranate on the ground and let nature take its course. Once the seeds germinate, transplant your bush into a spot where you want it to grow. Pomegranates planted close together make a great hedge plant.

Find a plant that produces a lot of fruit if that is your goal. Some varieties do not produce fruit well and are grown simply as ornamental plants. Generally, plants with double flowers will not produce much fruit. The pomegranate is one of those plants that lazy gardeners and devoted gardeners both adore. It is beautiful, productive, dramatic, and easy. Old as the hills, this lovely heirloom continues to surprise us with its versatility.

Creamy Cheesecake with Pomegranate Topping
Crust
    1 cup graham cracker crumbs (about 9 5-inch × 2.5-inch crackers)
    2 Tbsp. sugar
    ¼ cup unsalted butter, softened
Filling
    2 8-ounce containers whipped cream cheese
    3 large eggs
    ½ cup sugar
    2 Tbsp. orange-flavored liqueur
    ½ tsp. finely grated fresh orange zest

Topping
  Seeds from 2 pomegranates
  ¼ cup water
  ⅓ cup pomegranate juice
  1 tsp. unflavored gelatin
  2 Tbsp. sugar

Preheat oven to 350°F.

In a 9½-inch springform pan place crust ingredients and with fingers blend until combined well. Press mixture evenly over bottom and ¾ inch up side of pan.

In a large bowl with an electric mixer beat filling ingredients on high speed until light and fluffy, about 5 minutes. Pour filling into crust and bake in middle of oven 20 minutes, or until cheesecake is just set in center. (Cake will continue to set as it cools.)

Transfer cake in pan to a rack and cool, about 3 hours.

Place juice in a 1-cup liquid measure and add water. Sprinkle gelatin over pomegranate juice and let stand 1 minute to soften gelatin. Remove the seeds from the pomegranates.

Transfer gelatin mixture to a small saucepan. Add sugar and cook over moderate heat, stirring, until sugar is dissolved.

Pour mixture into a bowl and set bowl in a larger bowl of ice and cold water, stirring mixture gently until it is cold and slightly thickened but not set. Stir in pomegranate seeds and spoon topping onto chilled cheesecake.

Chill cake until topping is set, about 1 hour. Remove side of pan and serve chilled.

Passion Flower

The first time I was personally acquainted with a passion flower was when I found a straggly looking vine growing on a dilapidated fence on a dusty vacant lot in south Austin, Texas. I didn't even know what it was. The whole plant looked starved for water. The leaves were hanging down in a dejected way, but the flower was that unique and incredibly complex combination of various layers and different colors and textures heading off in different directions that characterizes the passion flower.

Passion flowers (*Passiflora*) come in a variety of colors and plant types. The most common color is blue purple, but there are yellow, red, and hues in between. A few passion flower plants are shrubs, but most are vines, and the species is found throughout the world except Antarctica and Africa. Nine species are native to the United States. Because the flowers produce seed pods that pop and scatter the seeds, they can easily become wild and grow in uncultivated places like that vacant lot.

During the fifteenth and sixteenth centuries Spanish Christian missionaries used the parts of this plant to symbolize and explain the last days (the passion) of Jesus: The pointed tips of the leaves were taken to represent the Holy Lance; the tendrils represent the whips used in the flagellation of Jesus; the ten petals and sepals represent the ten faithful apostles; the flower's radial filaments, which can number more than a hundred and vary from flower to flower, represent the crown of thorns; the chalice-shaped ovary represents the Holy Grail; the three stigmata represent the three nails and the five anthers below them the five wounds; and blue and white colors of many species' flowers represent Heaven and purity. The flower has many common names that reflect this association: Christ's thorn, Christ's crown, Christ's bouquet, crown of thorns, and others.

They also have such common names as maypop and clock plant. Maypop is native to the southeastern United States and has been grown as far north as Boston. It produces a sweet, edible, yellowish fruit about the size of an egg. The juice of the maypop is a good source of vitamins A and C. Simply cut the fruit in half, remove the seeds, and scoop out the meat. Add it to a fruit salad, make a juice or syrup from it, or just snack on it. Jams and jellies can also be made from passion fruit. You can com-

bine a puree of the fruit with other juices or teas to make refreshing iced summer beverages.

Maypop has a long history of use among Native Americans as a medicinal herb used to treat insomnia, hysteria, and epilepsy and as a painkiller. Studies are being done to find ways this plant can be used medicinally to treat many disorders. All of the above-ground parts of the passion vine plant can be brewed into a soothing, sleep-inducing tea. To make the sedative tea, put 1 teaspoon dried leaves into a pot and add 1 cup boiling water. Steep for 10 minutes and drink before bedtime. But don't drink the tea if you are pregnant.

Passion flower is a beautiful plant in the garden. Since I met that first pitiful specimen, I've seen and grown many vines that grow quickly and flower generously. You can buy plants or start them from seed. In most areas the plant will die down in the winter and come back up in the spring. It doesn't take long before the vine is covering your wall, fence, or whatever structure you give it to grow on.

Butterflies and hummingbirds and bees love the passion flower vine as much as people do. Hummingbirds, bumble bees, wasps, bats, and butterflies all pollinate the flowers, and the plants are an important source of nectar for many insects. In my area the fritillary butterfly dearly loves to lay its eggs on the leaves, which then feed its young. To prevent the butterflies from laying too many eggs on a single plant, some passion flowers bear small colored nibs that resemble butterfly eggs and seem to encourage some butterflies to move on.

I've found that the caterpillars don't really eat up the plant until it's about time for it to die back in the winter anyway. If you think there is too much chewing going on, you can remove by hand some of the caterpillars and put them on another plant. The butterflies are so lovely that it is a shame to discourage them, and the passion vine is so vigorous that you really don't have to worry much about it.

Plant your passion flower in good, well-draining soil and you will be rewarded with more and larger flowers. Although it will survive poor soil, it won't be nearly as pretty as it will if you add compost and minerals to your soil. It will thrive in full sun or partial shade but does like a reliable source of water—either rain or the hose. You need to provide support on which the vine can grow—a fence or trellis is great. You can also plant your passion flower in a large container if you don't have a spot in the garden. The plants are rarely bothered by pests or diseases.

My older daughter Sarah has inherited my love of plants and gardens. Being an army wife, however, makes growing a long-term garden much more difficult. Still, she perseveres. And the earth benefits from her efforts. Every time she moves, she leaves behind a little haven of beautiful and sturdy plants. Just because you have to leave behind a garden doesn't mean that your efforts are wasted. Her new home is now being transformed from a nice lawn of grass and shrubs into a home for all sorts of people and critters. Vegetable beds have been dug; flowers have been planted, and a new passion flower vine is making its way up the trellis just outside the bedroom window.

Trumpet Vine

Another one of my favorite vines is the orange trumpet vine (*Campsis radicans*). Also called trumpet creeper and cow itch vine, this plant is an example of how sturdy and determined old plants can be. I got my first start of this woody vine from downtown Austin, where it apparently was growing in concrete and climbing up a telephone pole. I simply snipped

off a section of vine and stuck it in some dirt, and it grew. I took my cue from its habitat and planted it to grow up a wire holding up a light pole in my front yard in the country. I've moved from that home now, but when I pass by I see that the vine is still going—up and up and out and out. Once it gets established, trumpet vine needs absolutely no care at all. It will make thick, branchlike stems and dense foliage. It is a favorite of birds who like to hide their nests in the complex of leaves and stems and tendrils. It will grab hold of almost anything in reach, so be careful. It will happily sneak in to weak arbors and fences and knock them right down. Be sure to plant it on a sturdy support. The beautiful trumpet-shaped flowers grow in clusters and are beloved by hummingbirds. The vine may die down in cold winters, but it will pop back up as soon as the weather warms and take off. It gets bigger every year.

The plant I have now came from my mother's yard. I went back a couple of years ago to wander on the vacant lot where her house had stood. I'd grown up in that house and loved it dearly. It burned to the ground some years after she moved on, but the lot sat vacant for some time. I found this straggly little vine growing at the back of the lot. At first I thought it was a wisteria vine, but once it got started in my garden, it was obviously a trumpet vine. It's growing now on my gazebo and keeping me and the hummingbirds happy.

Trumpet vine will grow in poor soil in zones 3–9 and in full sun or partial shade. It is easy and adaptable to the point of being a pest in some areas. Be sure you leave it room to spread when you plant it. But it is a beautiful cover for a fence, arbor, or trellis in areas where you don't want to have to give a plant a lot of attention. It is self-sufficient and extremely easy to propagate. You can take a cutting as I did or collect seeds in the late fall or early winter. These seeds are winged to blow in the wind and plant themselves. So if you don't want more trumpets, pick them before Mother Nature does!

CHAPTER 7

Mixing It Up

The list of wonderful heirloom plants is almost endless. Cultural groups, geographic locations, families, and neighborhoods all have their favorites. The wonderful diversity offered by heirloom plants can help you create a deeply satisfying garden that looks good, preserves historic plants, and provides you with color, shade, food, flowers, herbs, and an all-around happy place.

The best gardens are those that contain many different kinds of plants and that encourage life, whether it be human or otherwise. Heirloom plants allow you to combine vines, trees, vegetables, and more into easy-to-maintain, easy-to-propagate diversity. There is no reason why roses or herbs should be segregated into their own little gardens. Mix up your heirlooms; add a few new favorites and create a haven all your own.

Thank You

To gardeners everywhere who keep these treasures going and share them with others. And to the readers of *Homegrown* who kept me going.

To my family who continue to encourage and inspire: Bob Helberg, who travels tirelessly with me from garden to garden; Sarah Chance, who proofreads and helps with all kinds of technological conundrums; Jenny Turner, who proofreads and makes intelligent suggestions; and my wonderful grandchildren, who give me hope for the future of the garden and the earth. I also want to thank my mother, who gave me a love of plants and encouraged me to dig in the dirt at an early age. She also taught me that being a haphazard gardener isn't always a bad thing.

Appendix A

THE MILLENNIUM SEED BANK PROJECT

Plants are useful in cleaning the air and the water and in providing fuel, fiber, resins, food, and medicine. They also play a vital role in combating climate change and keeping the environment healthy. But today between sixty thousand and one hundred thousand species of plants are threatened with extinction—roughly a quarter of all plant species. Plants are dying out primarily as a result of the clearing of native vegetation, overexploitation, and climate change.

In response to this crisis, in 2000 the Royal Botanic Gardens at Kew in England and partner groups in fifty countries established the Millennium Seed Bank to save potentially valuable varieties. The Lady Bird Johnson Wildflower Center in Austin, Texas, was the first nongovernmental group asked to join the project. The bank's collection of seeds, located in England, is seen as an "insurance policy" against the extinction of plants in the wild. In April 2007 it banked its billionth seed, and its goal is to save seeds of 25 percent of the world's wild plant species by 2020. The project targets plants seen as most useful for the future including those in areas most at risk for climate change and impact of human activities. The public is able to help in the effort by contacting a local participant or going to Kew Garden's adopt-a-seed website: http://www.kew.org/support-kew/adopt-a-seed/index.htm.

Appendix B

SAFE SEX FOR COMMON GARDEN PLANTS

If you want to save seeds in your home garden, you have to consider the issue of cross-pollination. Crossing will result in seeds that will produce fruit unlike that of the parent.

The following crops do not readily cross, and more than one variety may be grown at a time:

- Common beans. Includes pinto, kidney, string, wax, and so on.
- Peas. Be extra careful in labeling, as many varieties are very similar in appearance.
- Tomatoes. Although they don't cross readily, it's best not to plant two varieties side by side.
- Potatoes. Asexually reproduced; no danger of crossing.
- Garlic. Asexually reproduced; no danger of crossing

The following crops do readily cross-pollinate. Raise only one variety of each or separate them as far as possible by distance combined with barriers (buildings, trees, tall crops). Be prepared for a noticeable (but mostly acceptable for home use) rate of crossing.

- Carrots will cross with each other and with Queen Anne's lace.
- Corn crosses between sweet corn and flour, flint, or pop varieties are not acceptable. Crosses between one sweet corn and another are okay.
- Lettuce may possibly cross with wild lettuces as well as with other cultivated varieties.
- Lima bean varieties will cross among themselves but not with other kinds of beans.

- Onions will cross with other onions but not with leeks or chives.
- Peppers will cross between sweet and hot varieties. The resultant pepper will almost always be hot.
- Radishes will cross; small salad and large oriental types will combine for a mess.
- Spinach will cross-pollinate for long distances because of wind-borne pollen.
- Sunflower hybrids will cross with wild sunflowers.
- Cantaloupes will cross among varieties and also with honeydew, casaba and Crenshaw melons.
- Cucumbers will cross with other cucumbers. Armenian cucumber is actually a melon and will cross with other melons.
- Watermelons will cross among varieties and with citron melons.
- Gourds will cross with other varieties.

Note: Cantaloupes, watermelons, gourds, squashes, and cucumbers will not cross-pollinate with each other.

There are four distinct species of squash. Crosses do occur within species but are rare between different species. For raising seed, select one of each species and you may still grow four different pure seed strains per year. Separate the four anyway to control the spread of disease and insects. The four varieties of *Cucurbita pepo* include acorn, yellow summer, zucchini, patty pan, and jack-o'-lantern squashes and small ornamental gourds. *Cucurbita maxima* include Hubbard, banana, and turban squashes. *Cucurbita moschata* includes butternut, cheese, Tahitian melon, and golden cushaw squashes. *Cucurbita mixta* includes all cushaws except golden. Hand pollination of squash is the alternative to separation. Check a book on pollination to learn the technique.

Plant Isolation Distances

The following distances are recommended by Suzanne Ashworth of Seed Savers Exchange and the U.S. Department of Agriculture. Generally, Ashworth recommends longer distances.

PLANT	ASHWORTH	USDA	POLLINATOR
Amaranth, Green	¼ mile	—	wind, insects
Amaranth, Grain	2 miles	—	wind, insects
Arugula	½ mile	660 feet	insects
Basil	150 feet	—	insects
Bean, Common	0–1 mile*	0	self
Bean, Fava	0–1 mile*	0	self
Bean, Lima	0–1 mile*	0	self
Bean, Tepary	0–1 mile*	0	self
Beet	5 miles	—	wind
Broccoli	1 mile	660 feet	insects
Broomcorn	—	660 feet	self
Brussels Sprouts	1 mile	660 feet	insects
Cabbage	1 mile	660 feet	insects
Cantaloupe	½ mile	¼ mile	insects
Carrot	¼ mile	—	insects
Cauliflower	1 mile	660 feet	insects
Celery	1 mile	—	insects
Chinese Cabbage	1 mile	660 feet	insects
Chinese Mustard	1 mile	660 feet	insects
Chives	1 mile	¼ mile	insects
Collards	1 mile	660 feet	insects
Cilantro	1/4 mile	—	insects
Corn	2 miles	660 feet	wind
Cowpea	0–1 mile*	0	self
Cucumber	½ mile	¼ mile	insects
Dill	1 mile	—	insects
Eggplant	50 feet	—	self
Fennel	½ mile	—	insects
Garlic chives	1 mile	¼ mile	insects
Gourds	½ mile	¼ mile	insects
Kale	½ mile	660 feet	insects

Lettuce	25 feet	—	self
Melon, Honeydew	½ mile	¼ mile	insects
Mustard	½ mile	660 feet	insects
Okra	1 mile	825 feet	self, insects
Onion	1 mile	¼ mile	insects
Parsley	1 mile	—	insects
Pea	50 feet	0	self
Pepper	500 feet	30 feet	self, insects
Pumpkin	½ mile	¼ mile	insects
Radish	½ mile	660 feet	insects
Spinach	5 miles	—	wind
Squash	½ mile	¼ mile	insects
Sunflower	½–3 miles	½ mile	insects
Swiss Chard	5 miles	—	wind
Tomatillo	0-?*	30 feet	self
Tomato	0-?*	30 feet	self
Turnip	1 mile	660 feet	insects
Watermelon	½ mile	¼ mile	insects

*These plants are self-pollinating and do not usually require isolation between varieties.

Appendix C

SOURCES FOR HEIRLOOM PLANTS AND SEEDS

Remember, always shop locally first. Encourage your local nurseries to carry heirloom seeds and plants and support their doing so by buying them. If enough people look for them, the nurseries will demand them and growers will grow them. There are many old varieties now in nurseries because of the growing interest in these old plants. Don't ask a commercial nursery if they will give you a cutting, seed or whatever. They are in business to sell plants, and if you want them to continue in business, support their efforts by buying their plants. Local nurseries are an invaluable resource for gardeners, and they are fighting an uphill battle with big box stores, the internet, and catalogs. Keep them going! They are worth it.

Plant fairs, herb fairs, garden shows, and other events where plants are for sale are a good opportunity to find old, unusual plants. Many garden clubs have events where their members bring cuttings from their own gardens. This is a great chance to see what's available in your town.

Shop your neighbors' yards as well. Older gardens are especially good snooping grounds, and most gardeners are happy to share—especially if you volunteer to do the work of dividing the plants or harvesting the seeds. Don't just help yourself. Always ask the property owner if you can have a cutting or seed or whatever. You might also offer to trade something you have for something another gardener has. Setting up a plant swap can be lots of fun and rewarding as well.

Join a seed savers organization. You can learn about plants, seeds, and seed saving through their booklets and newsletters. You can also find out about other seed savers in your area and what plants they have to offer. When you join a seed saving group, you have the option of either offering seeds or acquiring seeds, or you can do both. Generally you pay for postage for mailing the seeds, and that's all. It is a great way to find some wonderful old plants that are not available commercially.

National seed savers groups offer a wide selection of seeds. Be sure, however, that you get those that are adapted to your own growing conditions. An old Amish variety that does great in Pennsylvania won't necessarily do well in South Texas.

If you can't find what you want locally, check out mail order catalogs. Many have online sites, and others have nice paper catalogs. Look for the plants that originated in the area where you live or in areas where the conditions are similar to yours.

Of course, experimentation is at the heart of gardening. If you see a plant that calls your name, give it a try. Who knows, it might be the next great garden treasure!

National Seed Exchanges

Seed Savers Exchange, Rt. 3 Box 239, Decorah, IA 52101; 563–382–5990; http://www.seedsavers.org

Southern Exposure Seed Exchange, P.O. Box 460, Mineral, VA 23117; 540–894–9480; http://www.southernexposure.com

Regional Seed Exchanges

Appalachian Heirloom Seed Conservancy, Box 519, Richmond, KY 40476; KentuckySeeds@hotmail.com

CORNS Seed Exchange, c/o Carl Barnes, R.R. 1, Box 32, Turpin, OK 73950

Garden State Heirloom Seed Society, P.O. Box 15, Valley Road, Delaware, NJ 07833

Maine Seed Saving Network, P.O. Box 126, Penobscot, ME 04476; 207–326–0751

Ozark Seed Exchange, 33018 Hwy 123, Hagarville, AR 72839, dcoda@ozarkseedexchange.com

Southern Seed Legacy Project, 104A Baldwin Hall, Department of Anthropology, University of Georgia, Athens, GA 30605

Abundant Life Seed Foundation, P.O. Box 279, Cottage Grove, WA
    97424; 541–767–9606; http://www.abundantlifeseeds.com

Antique Rose Emporium, 9300 Lueckemeyer Rd., Brenham, TX 77833;
    800–441–0002; http://www.antiqueroseemporium.com

Antique Rose Farm, 12220 Springhetti Rd., Snohomish, WA 98296;
    360–568–1919; http://www.antiquerosefarm.com

Antique Rose Gardens, 5716 Main Hwy, St. Martinsville, LA; 337–394–
    8877; http://www.antiquerosegardens.com

Baker Creek Heirloom Seeds, 2278 Baker Creek Rd., Mansfield, MO
    65704; 417–924–8917; http://www.rareseeds.com

Bountiful Gardens, 18001 Shafer Ranch Rd., Willits, CA 95490; 707–
    459–6410; http://www.bountifulgardens.org

Burpee Seeds, 300 Park Avenue, Warminster, PA 18991; 800–333–5808;
    http://www.burpee.com

Chamblees Roses, 10926 U.S. Hwy 69N, Tyler, TX 75706; 800–256-7673;
    http://www.chambleeroses.com

Colonial Williamsburg: The Colonial Nursery Seed List, The Colonial
    Nursery, P.O. Box 1776, Williamsburg, VA 23187–1776; http://www.
    history.org/History/CWLand//nursery1.cfm

Fedco Seeds, P.O. Box 520, Waterville, ME 04903; 207–873–7333; http://
    www.fedcoseeds.com

Filaree Farm, 182 Conconully Highway, Okanogan, WA 87740, 509–422–
    6940; http://www.filareefarm.com

George's Plant Farm, 1410 Public Wells Road, Martin, TN 38237, 731–
    587–9477; http://www.tatorman.com. Sweet potato slips

Heirloom Seeds, online only; http://www.heirloomseeds.com

Heirloom Tomatoes, 5423 Princess Drive, Rosedale, MD 21237; http://
    www.heirloomtomatoes.net

Irish Eyes—Garden City Seeds, P.O. Box 307, Thorp, WA 98946; 509–
    964–7000; http://www.gardencityseeds.net. Garlic, potatoes, and seeds

Johnny's Selected Seeds, 955 Benton Avenue, Winslow, ME 04901;
    209–861–3999. http://www.johnnyseeds.com

D. Landreth Seed Company, 60 East High Street, Bldg #4, New Freedom,
    PA 17340; 800–654–2407; http://www.landrethseeds.com

Native Seeds/SEARCH, 2509 N. Campbell #325, Tucson, AZ 85719; http://www.nativeseeds.org

Nichols Garden Nursery, 1190 Old Salem Rd. NE, Albany, OR 97321; 800–422–3985; http://www.gardennursery.com

Old House Gardens, 536 Third St., Ann Arbor, MI 48103; 734–995–1486; http://www.oldhousegardens.com

Old Sturbridge Village Seed Store, 1 Old Sturbridge Village Rd., Sturbridge, MA 01566; 508–347–0244; http://www.osv.org

Organica Seed Co., P.O. Box 611, Wilbraham, MA 01095: http://www.organicaseed.com

Pinetree Garden Seeds, Box 300, New Gloucester, ME 04260; 207–926–3400; http://www.superseeds.com

Plants of the Southwest, 3095 Aqua Fria, Santa Fe, NM 87507; 800–778–7333; http://www.plantsofthesouthwest.com

Plimoth Plantation, 137 Warren Avenue, Plymouth, MA 02360; http://www.plimoth.com

Renee's Garden Seeds, 6116 Highway 9, Felton, CA 95018; 888–880–7228; http://www.reneesgarden.com

Ronniger Potato Farm, 12101 2135 Rd., Austin, CO 81410; 877–204–8704; http://www.ronnigers.com. Potatoes

Sand Hill Preservation Center, 1878 230th Street, Calamus, IA 52729; http://www.sandhillpreservation.com. Seeds, poultry, sweet potato slips

Seeds of Change, P.O. Box 15700, Santa Fe, NM 87506; 888–762–7333; http://www.seedsofchange.com

Select Seeds, 108 Stickney Hill Rd., Union, CT 06076; 800–684–0395; http://www.selectseeds.com

Seminole Springs Antique Rose and Herb Farm, 34935 Huff Rd., Eustis, FL 32736; 352–357–2643; http://www.rosesandherbs.com

R. H. Shumway's, 334 W. Stroud St., Randolph, WI 53956; 800–342–9461; http://www.rhshumway.com

Skyfire Garden Seeds, 1313 23rd Road, Kanopolis, KS 67454; http://www.skyfiregardenseeds.com

South Carolina Foundation Seed Association, 1162 Cherry Road, Box 349952, Clemson, SC 29634; 864–656–2520; http://virtual.clemson.edu/groups/seed/heirloom.htm

Thomas Jefferson Center for Historic Plants, Monticello, P.O. Box 316, Charlottesville, VA 22902; 800–243–1743; http://www.monticellocatalog.org/outdoor---garden-plants---seeds.html

Tomato Growers Supply, P.O. Box 60015, Fort Myers, FL 33906; 888–478–7333; http://www.tomatogrowers.com

Vermont Bean Seed Company, 334 West Stroud Street, Randolph, WI 53956; 800–349–1071; http://www.vermontbean.com

Victory Seed Company, P.O. Box 192, Molalla, OR 97038; 503–829–3126; http://www.victoryseeds.com

Wayside Gardens, 1 Garden Lane, Hodges, SC 29695; 800–213–0379; http://www.waysidegardens.com

Yucca Do Nursery, P.O. Box 1039, Giddings, TX 78942; 979–542–8811; http://www.yuccado.com

Index

tomatoes, 7, 9, 10, 11, 15, 20, 21:
    Cherokee purple, 15, 20, 24; German
tomatoes (*cont.*)
    Johnson, 15; Italian rose, 23;
    persimmon, 24; Porter, 25; yellow
    pear, 25
trumpet vine, 12, 121

verbena, 8

vitex, 12
Washington, George, 106
What Can I Do With My Herbs? 95
winter vegetable soup, 77

yams, 60
yellow bells (*Tecoma stans*), 12

zinnia, 4, 88

W. L. Moody Jr. Natural History Series

World of the Harvester Ants, Stephen W. Taber

Grasses of the Texas Gulf Prairies and Marshes, Stephan L. Hatch, Joseph L. Schuster, and D. Lynn Drawe

Amphibians and Reptiles of Texas, Second Edition, James R. Dixon

Marine Mammals of the Gulf of Mexico, Bernd Würsig, Thomas A. Jefferson, and Dave J. Schmidly

On Bobwhites, Fred S. Guthery

American Aquarium Fishes, Robert J. Goldstein, Rodney W. Harper, and Richard Edwards

Birds of the Texas Panhandle, Kenneth D. Seyffert

Birds of the Southwest: Arizona, New Mexico, Southern California, & Southern Nevada, John Rappole

The Snakes of Trinidad and Tobago, Hans E. A. Boos

Birds of Northeast Texas, Matt White

Insects of the Texas Lost Pines, Stephen W. Taber and Scott B. Fleenor

Trees of Texas: An Easy Guide to Leaf Identification, Carmine A. Stahl and Ria McElvaney

Birding the Southwestern National Parks, Roland H. Wauer

What Can I Do With My Herbs, Judy Barrett